300+ CRAPPIE FISHING TIPS

Featuring Charles & Travis Bunting

Tim Huffman

300+ CRAPPIE FISHING TIPS

Featuring Charles & Travis Bunting

Print version: ISBN 978-0-9989089-1-5

CHARLES AND TRAVIS BUNTING are winners of three national championships and the only team to win National Championship Classics in all three major circuits. They've won a points championship, along with regional and state titles. The team has a sincere desire to help others catch fish so they do many seminars and events each year. Their wrapped boat draws a lot of attention, so they answer questions at baitshops, gas stations and motels, too. They are experienced on waters from Florida to Indiana, the Carolinas to Oklahoma and many in between. Their knowledge and experience qualify them as perfect experts for this book of tips, tactics, gear and presentations.

TABLE OF CONTENTS

DEDICATION

A man is indeed blessed when he has a wife, soul mate, best friend and beautiful Christian woman to share his life and dreams. I thank you, Jeanne, for being all of that and more.

CHAPTER 1
JIGGING ... WOOD COVER, TECHNIQUE & DEPTHS

Jigging is easy. A fisherman needs basic gear and the physical ability to hold a pole for an extended period of time.

Jigging receives high marks for low cost. Required items are a pole, basic reel, line and a few jigs. A simple boat with a trolling motor will work fine. A big, heavy boat gives more stability, but a lightweight johnboat is better for getting in and around cover.

Charlie Bunting says, "I rate jig fishing as the easiest to learn and perform. It's an easy way to fish because you are basically dipping vertically. You need a sensitive pole and a few jigs. It's one of my favorite ways to fish."

A lake's quality as prime jigging water is often directly proportional to its cover and depths. Bowl-type lakes with little or no cover are better suited for multiple-pole trolling techniques. Crappie in deep water can be jigged, but jigging becomes more difficult and less efficient as depths increase, especially over 15 feet. So the ideal water is 12 feet or less with lots of visible and submerged cover.

JIGGING ... WOOD COVER

Call it jigging, vertical jigging, one-poling, dipping, dabbling or whatever else you want to call a single long pole, hand-held, vertical presentation.

One of the Buntings' home waters is Truman Lake in Missouri. It's a jig fisherman's dream with thousands of acres of standing timber, stumps and laydowns. In addition, fishermen have placed stakebeds and other covers to sweeten spots and areas. There are seldom jet skis or water skiers in fishing areas due to timber.

Fishing with them at Truman was an advanced crash course in vertical jigging. The team says the following tips apply to Reelfoot, Conway, Lake Fork and any similar waters.

Travis says, "Fishing stumps, snags, trees and laydowns is some of the most fun we have all year long. It's a great way to catch crappie. We are versatile and like all techniques, but jigging is fun. Spring is a prime time across the country, but other seasons can be good, too.

"The advantage of jigging is that it gets a bait into places you can't get it with other methods. It's a straight up and down presentation with some pitching and swimming where limbs allow. Different depths can be fished, and the bait can be held still or jigged."

1 Travis says, "When there are many acres of water with wood, it can all look the same. Therefore, take a close look at the wood types. When you catch a few fish, look for differences in wood, maybe a double tree versus single, a hedge versus a hardwood.

2 "Watch bottom depths and contours. A one-foot drop can be important. Crappie prefer a little contour difference along with wood cover. Don't ignore the depths and drops just because you are fishing wood."

Charles agrees that a little difference in bottom can be important. "Pay attention. A good tip for fishing a massive forest of

wood in a lake is to look for a contour and for bottom hardness. If you catch fish on the same trees every time you fish them, pay attention to the bottom near those trees. There may be something different that attracts the crappie to those particular trees."

3 Travis says, "A lot of trees, like a hardwood or hedge, last a long time, but the tree will rot off just above the surface. The top is still there but usually it's at the base or near the tree. The tree is good fishing, but the submerged top might be better. So don't forget to look and fish away from the tree. You might catch fish on the tree and on the brushy stuff next to it.

4 "Just because there are many trees doesn't mean that stakebeds aren't important. There are three theories to using stakebeds with trees. The first theory is to create a big base at the bottom of the tree. This increases the size of the bottom of the trunk and adds small stickups along with the big trunk. That's a good combination.

5 "The second bed tactic is to place a bed 10 to 20 feet away from the tree or trees," says Travis. "Crappie will still come to the bed, but fishermen concentrating on the trees won't find the bed. The bed remains close enough to turn around, fish the opposite side of the boat and to fish the bed without moving the boat. With today's electronics and other fishermen watching, you can't hide it, but the average fisherman will likely never find it.

"If you place a bed 10 yards away from a good, productive tree like a hedge, one day the fish might be in the hedge and the next day in the bed, but they are usually not on both. So don't give up if fish aren't on the first one you try because they might be loaded on something right next to it.

6 "The third theory is to place beds 30 yards or more away from the trees," says Travis." Most beds will still draw fish from the trees, but fewer fishermen will find and fish them. Sometimes these beds are great and sometime, for some reason, fish don't like them."

7 Charles says, "Tree types can be important. In summertime, the June through August period, we are looking for hedge and cedar trees here at Truman. After temperatures start dropping, fish will leave and go to different hardwoods. Middle to late fall we've learned that the bigger stumps hold the bigger fish.

"Crappie will change patterns with seasonal or weather changes. Hardwoods, singles, doubles, triples and small stuff around them are choices. Doubles usually do better than singles. Above the water you might see one tree but on the locator you might see a double or triple, what we call a 'crappie fork' down at three feet under the water. Other fishermen will be passing to hit visible multiples, but the underwater ones have very little pressure."

JIGGING ... BY DEPTH ZONES

Shallow Water (0-5 Feet)

Travis says, "Truman Lake breaks all the rules because some of the best shallow-water fishing happens in June, July and August. That's very different than most waters. Typically, the shallow bite in most lakes drops off dramatically when the water heats up.

8 "This proves the fact that no water should be eliminated until fished. Improved efficiency and increased number of fishermen on the lakes has removed most of the secrets, but fish are still fish and they don't read books of tips. So it's best to stay open-minded to look elsewhere when your favorite spots aren't producing.

9 "We like fishing shallow water. There are many advantages. Never overlook the shallow water. Shallow water is the easiest to fish. A fisherman has less water to fish so crappie can be found quicker than in deep water.

10 "Stained water is very important for good fishing. Water too clear means the crappie will be spooky. We look for stained water because it's easier to fish and often has bigger fish."

Mid-Depths (6-14 Feet in Stained Water)

Middle depths are very good in most of the seasons, but depth, water color and clarity all play a role.

11 Charles says, "Prespawn fish will start deep, move up to the mid-depths covers and then move up into the shallows. The fish reverse the process after the spawn. The fish, at least some of them, will move from shallow water out to the mid-depths after the spawn.

12 "Many of the fish that move to the mid-depths will suspend up in the upper part of the water column. Crappie may be three feet deep in 10 feet of water."

Deep Water (15 Feet & Deeper)

"Fish can be caught year-round by vertical jigging," says Charles. "However, we seldom fish over 12 feet deep so we seldom jig in deep water. Also, many of our fishing trips are for prefishing and tournaments. We struggle to keep fish alive if they are caught deeper than 15 feet deep. We like shallower depths and they are required for our tournament fishing."

JIGGING ... THE TECHNIQUE

Equipment

Charles says, "There are many good poles on the market. BnM Pole Company is one of our sponsors, but I would fish those poles anyway. We like the 12-foot Ultra-Lite because it is so sensitive and lightweight. The sensitivity means we feel more bites. A lightweight pole is less tiring, and that's important."

13 He says a pole needs to be very sensitive. It is the one common characteristic all fishermen agree upon. More fish will be caught if a fisherman feels more bites.

14 Under-the-forearm models, with the reel seat up 12 to 16 inches from the butt of the pole, are good for hoisting crappie up and out of the water.

A rear-seat-type handle gives great feel and balance. Using an under-the-forearm or a rear-seat model is a personal choice based upon how a fisherman likes to hold a jigging pole.

15 Pole lengths might be as short as nine feet in stained water with overhanging limbs. In deep water, a short pole gives good bait control, and getting away from the boat isn't important.

A pole can be 14- or 16-feet long to reach spots and to use when fish are spooky, but for practical jigging, a 12-foot pole is the maximum length because of weight. Arm fatigue becomes a factor if the pole is too long. An 11-foot pole is common.

16 Charlie says, "We like braided line. Jigging is the only technique that we prefer braid. The braid is strong and sensitive, giving an advantage in resistance to wear, and we feel more bites. We use Vicious 10/2 High-Visibility Braid."

Travis agrees. "We use braid when jigging because the sensitivity lets us feel more bites and we lose fewer fish. When using mono, we would catch five fish, but then the sixth one would pop the line because of the wear on the line from the wood. We're often asked about braid in clear-water, but we've used it and caught fish. The boat will more likely spook clear water crappie than the line."

17 Charlie says, "I use one reel, the BnM Pro 100 spinning reel, for every technique including jigging. Other type reels work, but I recommend a spinning reel for crappie fishing. It is versatile and has a good drag."

18 Travis says, "Jigging can be done from small boats. You can do everything from a small boat, but safety requires picking spots and maybe the right days to fish.

We jig from a big Ranger boat because high wind conditions. A heavy boat is good for motoring or fishing in strong wind. With small boats, wind can become a safety issue. However, pick the right days and a smaller boat is fine. It can be an advantage in thick timber. A big 21- or 22-foot boat is fantastic in open water when shooting docks or fishing trees, it's not as good as a smaller boat."

Technique Presentation

Travis says, "At Truman we'll be fishing the trees. We'll likely be using a ¼-ounce jighead, and, for sure, the color will be orange. We use to have every color of jighead and have narrowed it down to orange as what works best for us."

He says the presentation depends upon the area and wood being fished, along with the aggressiveness of the fish. "For example, the thick top of a laydown might be jigged up and down to prevent hangups. However, a stump or an old standing tree might let us pitch past the wood and have it pendulum down. Pitching can be good for triggering strikes, but horizontal limbs will stop the fall.

19 "Whether jigging a fencerow or a big stump, presentations are a key element to being successful. One method is to work slow and methodical. When the water is deep, it takes a while to work from top to bottom. A snag needs to be worked from about a foot down all the way to the bottom. That takes time.

20 "The presentation is different after the strike zone is found. If the zone is three to four feet deep, then the jig can be quickly put into the strike zone without wasting time at non-productive depths. The jig may have to be left still for a while, but more likely the bite will be aggressive or hungry, or both, and each wood cover can be fished quickly.

21 "Slowing a bait down offers fish a chance to look at the bait. Even if that fish is not hungry, it will eventually take the bait if it's there long enough. That is super-slow jigging but works.

"Example, I will eat a piece of cherry or coconut cream pie if it's set in front of me, even if I'm not hungry. Why should a crappie be any different with a good-looking, sweet-smelling minnow or jig. Is it hungry? No. Will it eat? Usually yes."

22 Boat control is an important part of a presentation. The angle of attack should consider the wind as a major player in the approach. Wind, sun and current are factors the team considers before fishing a spot.

23 Travis says, "You have to start each day looking for the right depth. Just because they hit at three feet yesterday doesn't mean they'll be at that depth today. Maybe barometric pressure or light penetration changes their depth.

24 "Fishing is always changing. When you figure it out, it's important to continuing doing what works. Repeat, repeat, repeat to keep doing what's working.

25 "We jig in two different ways. We drop with a 1/16-ounce jig to see if they want to hit on a slow fall. And, we use a 1/8- or 1/4-ounce, drop to the bottom and work it slowly up all the way to the top.

26 "The slower the bite, the more you need to slow your presentation. To tell you the truth, I'll try almost anything when the bite is slow. I've even added rattles to my jig to try to draw more strikes.

27 "Swim a jig around a tree. It keeps the bait in the water and gives them a different look. A lot of times you'll have to lift the bait up and over underwater limbs, but that's okay.

28 "Use your off hand to control the bait. Grab your line and slide it with your off hand to work from low to high. You don't want the rod tip up in the air, especially on windy days. Also, you don't have a good hookset if the rod is up in the air.

29 "If fishing shallow water, I like to have more line out because if I only have three feet of line out and catch fish, then I have to let line out. I'm likely to lose the fish. Having extra line in my hand allows me to leave pressure on the fish while releasing the line, so I will have enough line to swing the fish in.

30 "I can fish 15 feet deep and never use the reel by pulling line with my off hand to shorten the line.

31 "Swinging the jig down in a pendulum motion lets the jig come to the fish at an angle. The fall angle can trigger a strike."

32 Charles says, "Use a bobber stop when jigging. Set it so it is at a specific depth, say four feet when fishing six feet of water. By knowing where your bobber stop is located when you are catching fish, you can get the bait to the right depth quick and accurate. Sometimes a difference of six inches can be critical."

Cabela's

CHAPTER 2
RUN & GUN JIGGING ...
THE AGGRESSIVE PRESENTATION

There is nothing slow and methodical about run-and-gun fishing. It basically means hitting as many spots as possible in a day of fishing. The focus is finding the most aggressive fish. Run-and-gun strategy can be great when trying to catch as many fish as possible when crappie are neutral or active.

Travis says, "The run-and-gun style of fishing depends upon the bite. It's for active or semi-active fish. We try to fish as many spots as possible looking for those fish. We don't sit on a tree waiting for a bite.

33 "When the bite is aggressive," continues Travis, "I'll leave my trolling motor on 40 percent and keep going. That's when fishing is fun. I know the fish are hitting on the first drop so there is no need to keep my jig in there for a long time. I hit stump after stump or tree after tree.

34 "We'll combine run-and-gun with slow down if fish are on a particular tree or type of cover. For example, we might blow into a cove, fish two specific trees we believe will hold crappie, then blow back out. However, we will slow our presentation while at those two trees. We fish slowly but only choose trees that the pattern has shown to hold fish.

35 "The biggest jigging tip I have for a beginner is to take the tie-up ropes out of the boat, throw them away and stay on the move. There are only so many fish around a spot, and only so many fish are going to eat. So keep moving and stop wasting time tying up and waiting on a bite.

36 "Run-and-gun means an aggressive fish, but they still might be finicky about the type bait and how it is presented. I get stuck on heavy baits. In shallow water a 1⁄16-ounce, or maybe even a 1⁄32-ounce, will give a slow presentation they love.

37 "Whether run-and-gun or not, I like to swim my jig around a stump instead of picking it up. Most fishermen pick it up so they won't get hung up. The crappie don't see the swim too often, so I catch a lot more fish. It just gives them a different look.

CHAPTER 3
JIGGING ... THE SEASONS, BAITS & BITES

SPRING

"We use big baits this time of year," says Travis. "We like our 2.5-inch Muddy Water bait or a big baby shad body. A big profile is important. We are power fishing this time of year so a big bait lets us go as fast as the fish will let us.

38 "Big baits allow fast presentations. When fish are aggressive, there is no reason to hold a jig in the spot for a long period of time, if hits are coming on the fall. Pitch the jig in, and if there is no bite when it stops, it's time to pull it out and move it.

39 "The jig body size is important, but so is the jighead weight. Aggressive fish will likely take a ¼-ounce head, or for sure a ⅛-ounce. A big head and body are not too big for a large crappie.

40 "When the bite is slow and fish are not aggressive, I like a 1.5-inch body. The fish might eat something small when they ignore a big bait.

41 "Until a pattern is formed, work methodically along a fence row, group of trees or whatever the lake has in it. The purpose is to form a pattern where you learn the depth, cover and presentation the fish like.

42 "Use a weedguard in heavy brush for fewer hangups. I don't use one when fishing moderate brush or open water."

43 Charles says, "Our favorite spring colors depend upon water colors. In clear water, we like white, blue and gold. In stained, we like a solid color like chartreuse glow that has pigment giving it a dark profile from below."

SUMMER JIGGING

"Summer jigging on Truman," says Charles, "will be on cedar trees most of the time. However, sometimes jigging is best on a different wood. Each day is a different trip, so we might have to look a while. When everybody says crappie are out in the deeper water, they mean the 9- to 11-inch crappie. You can catch them on the deeper trees. This is a good time of year for catching fish here at the lake. It's fun.

44 "The rule of thumb for speed is faster in spring but slower in summer. When working a small area with a jig, the bait needs to be presented slower. Less movement means more bites.

"Summer means all depths," says Charles. "Fish are scattered two to 12 feet here on our home lake. That can vary greatly if you fish other waters with many fish being very deep. A fisherman has to learn the range of the fish so he can learn the depth zone for the day.

45 "On a timber lake with a thermocline, it's easy because if fish are at eight feet, they'll be in eight or nine feet of water whether the water is 10 feet or 30 feet deep.

46 "There are times when you need to jig it, and there are times you have to deadstick and not move it. When taking the jig away, try swimming it away from the tree. I believe the fish sees the bait leaving the tree so it whacks it because he just can't resist."

JIGGING ... FALL

Charles says, "We jig all year-round. The shallower the water, the more we jig versus troll. As water cools in fall, you'll see fish get more aggressive, and the males make a fake spawning run back up toward shallow water.

47 "In fall we are looking for ledges at the top of the drop-offs and the timber. Or, cover on the ledges. If we spider rig, we will run down the ledges because the baitfish and crappie are on the ledges. The difference in single-pole jigging is that we are looking for specific spots to drop into.

48 "Jigging is all about being at the right depth. On cloudy days, look for fish to be high in the water column. The crappie will be deeper on sunny days."

BAITS & BITES

49 Charles Bunting says, "Jigging is best with a jig. You can work a jig any depth, in thicker cover and at a faster pace than you can with a minnow. Crappie like minnows, but sometimes they prefer a jig over a minnow. Most weekend fishermen are more comfortable with a minnow, at least a jig tipped with a minnow.

50 "There are other times a crappie wants a straight minnow and no jig. So that's what we will give them. Usually we will use a slip-cork to slow down and hit the right depth every time.

51 "A jig tipped with a minnow might be the best all-around jigging bait. It gives the color of the bait and real look and action of the minnow. Only by fishing different combinations will you learn what the crappie want on a particular day."

52 Travis says, "Crappie Masters has single-pole, artificial-bait-only tournaments. People gripe and complain, but the weights are often as good without minnows as with them. That tells me with more practice, more fishermen could catch about the same fish with a jig as with minnows when jigging.

53 "If I tip with a minnow, I like a medium, medium-large minnow. Their size is a 21-grade size and is about the same size a 2.5-inch jig.

54 "Jigging means that most bites will be felt. Only when the fish swims off to the side in shallow water is it easier to see than feel. The pole is in your hands so you should feel the bite.

55 "If you feel something or see line go slack on the fall, be sure to set the hook," says Travis. "It could be a limb, so you could lose your jig, but it's likely a fish. If you don't set the hook, you won't catch the fish.

56 "We fish fencerows a lot at Truman. On our trip today the fishing has been bad. At 11:00, it was like someone flipped a switch to 'On' and it's been non-stop action. It's not unusual to be a specific time every day for a week. The only thing I can figure out is the sun gets at the right angle to turn the fish on. The fish are there all day, so something triggers them to bite. Therefore, if you have an area where you've been catching fish, it's important to check it every hour or two. If you are not there when the fish turn on, you will miss the chance to catch them.

57 Travis and Charlie agree on setting the hook when you feel a bite. Travis says, "How long to wait to set the hook on a bite? Point zero, zero, zero seconds. Immediately. Delay and you've probably lost the opportunity for the fish.

"There is an exception in summer when fishing a split-shot and live minnow. You have to hold it. It might 'tic' the bait several times. It drives me crazy because I'm not patient. But slowly lift the bait up and, when the rod loads up, the fish has it so it's time to set the hook. If you set the hook before that, you'll never catch it."

JIGGING FACTORS

"Seldom is weather perfect," says Travis. "Even when it is stable, there is no guarantee the crappie will bite. I have to go fishing on my days off or for tournaments so I don't care if the wind is from the east or if a front is coming through or if it's snowing. I'm going fishing and will deal with whatever the weather is that day. There might be a reason the fish aren't active, but I don't like to use that as an excuse for not catching fish.

58 "Wind? A good ripple is good because it's more difficult for the fish to see shadows, the boat and fishermen.

59 "Jigging in strong wind? We will go with the wind in the stumps and snags. A fisherman can use Power Poles, chains or an anchor. We can drop our Power Poles before we get to the stump or tree. We won't have to make noise or throw backwash by using the trolling motor. We let the wind blow us then drop the poles to stop us exactly where we want. We're fishing immediately because the poles stop us and stabilize the boat. Plus, it's very quiet."

60 No Power Poles? "We know many fishermen don't have the Power Poles. For years we used chains to slow or stop the boat in the wind. They do the job but are a lot of work to pull in, out and adjust.

61 "A bright sun pulls the crappie tighter into the wood cover. I like sun in dingy water because crappie can see baits better," says Travis.

"Clouds are usually not good because it spreads the fish out. They don't need the cover to protect them from strong light penetration. The fish scatter. However, in clear water, the cloud cover can be good to break up shadows and silhouettes.

62 "Water color is important, but for getting bites, the color of the water isn't critical as long as it is stable. Water color becoming more stained or muddy due to rains is not good. We do a lot of searching to find the right water color. If water is stable, we'll be in the more stained water. Water color is also important for choosing the right jig colors.

63 "Fishing pressure can restrict where you can fish. The best places will likely have other fishermen on them. So fishing pressure never helps. How much it hurts depends upon the area and spots, and also the quality of fishermen fishing them.

64 "Cold fronts, especially in spring, aren't good. Fish won't bite well after a front, but by early summer, there are fewer fronts moving through.

"Cold fronts usually don't move fish away. They stay in the spot and just don't want to eat. It's important to be patient and give them time to bite after you drop a bait down to them."

65 Travis says, "I'm guessing 90 percent of the time we are swinging a fish into the boat instead of netting it. From the time you set the hook with a jigging pole until the fish hits the top of the water is a very limited time. By the time you let the fish flop around on top of the water waiting for the partner to set his pole down, get the net and get the net to the fish, it's too late. It's better to swing it in."

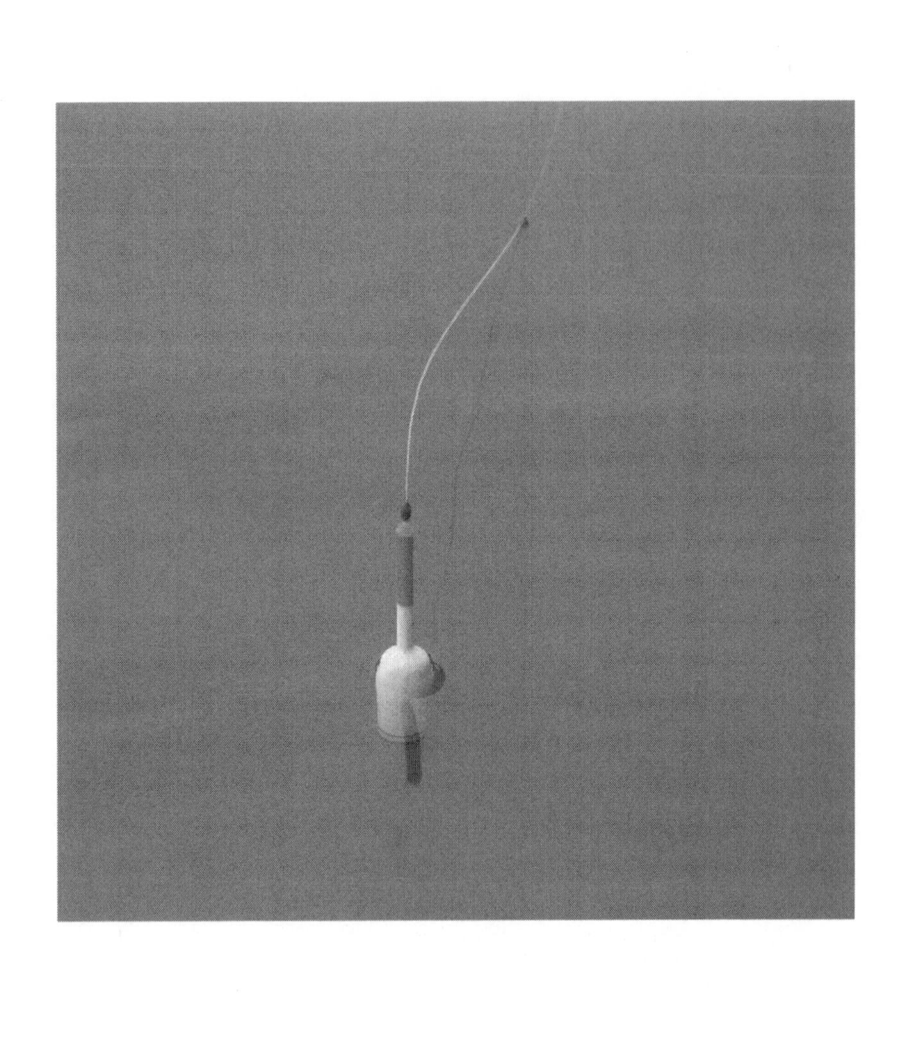

CHAPTER 4
PITCHING & CORKING

PITCHING

Charlie gives pitching a rating of 8 out of 10 if used in the right season. Learning and performing isn't difficult, and equipment costs are low.

"I will pitch, but I also use a bow-and-arrow style to shoot the bait so it's a little harder to do than jigging," says Charles. "I use a BnM 6-foot Sharpshooter. It's a new rod with a stiffer backbone, and it's at the top of its class. Travis might just pitch so a 7-foot rod is good for that."

Travis says, "Pitching and corking are two good methods. Pitching is without a float. It's easier to cover more water in a day when fishing a free-fall jig compared to using a float. The two tactics aren't much different except you have to control your depth by manually controlling the jig. Pitching lets a fisherman cover more depths in one pitch. Covering more depths per pitch can be a big advantage depending upon the situation.

"Pitching is how we learned to fish. That's how we started. It's a good technique, fun and very economical. It's an inexpensive method of fishing."

66 Travis explains, "A fisherman should use whatever pole is comfortable for pitching. I use a BnM 7-foot Sam Heaton to give me more control of the bait.

"The difference in a longer rod, say a 7-foot versus a 5.5-foot, is that after I hit structure, it's easier to pop it over the limbs with a longer rod. It also allows longer pitching.

"We like the rear-seat poles, too, like the Sam Heaton models, because of the balance and feel of the pole."

67 Charles says, "Our setup is simple, with our line being high-visibility monofilament, usually 6-pound-test. The high visibility is good because a lot of the time we see the bites instead of feel them. Light line gives good bait action.

68 "Choose a 1⁄32-, 1⁄16- or 3⁄32-ounce jig based upon the depth you are pitching. A light jig gives a good, slow fall and will trigger bites. A heavier jig gets deeper.

69 "When learning, I suggest staying with the same weight jig. That way a fisherman learns the fall rate of a jig and how it pendulums down.

70 Travis says, "We've discussed fall rate, but it's a critical part of pitching. I pay a lot of attention to the weight of my jig. The 1⁄16-ounce is enough weight to have control yet have a slow fall. If fish are just a little aggressive, I'll immediately switch to a 1⁄8-ounce or larger because they allow faster fishing.

71 "The difference in feel of a limb and a bite comes with experience. But in general, as your line comes over a limb, you'll feel tension. Next is a crisp 'tink' when the jig hits and comes over the limb and starts falling down. That's a limb."

Springtime Pitching

This is the obvious time for working the bank and structures near the bank. Pitching allows pinpoint precision and is a good way to work one to five feet, and anything in between. The water color usually will determine the depth of the fish. Therefore, you're prime target zone and spookiness of the fish will change based upon water color.

Travis says, "Fish move up to the shallow brush, the time most fishermen call crappie season. It's a great time to take your kids and grandkids fishing. It's easy to pitch and catch aggressive males off the bed. Targeting rocky banks can be good.

72 "Spring baits are usually chosen based upon the aggressiveness of the fish," says Travis. "A slow bite means a smaller jig. We've had good luck with the Southern Pro Rainbow jig. It's a small body with a good look.

73 "Will I put it in the brush? I target structure 90 percent of the time. If I can pitch to a brushpile, drag it through it and catch my limit of crappie, I'll do it. I might have to replace 10 or 15 jigs, stop to retie 10 or 15 times, but if I come home with a limit of fish because of the brush, versus not losing jigs and catching four crappie, it's the right thing to do. It blows my mind that a fisherman will spend money for truck fuel, boat fuel and all the other expenses, and yet worry about losing a 30-cent jig. We weren't pitching, but the worse day on hooks was losing 198 during a tournament. However, we won the tournament, so it was better to lose baits and catch fish."

74 Charlie states, "A good spring color is white-blue in clear water. In stained we want a chartreuse glow. This is true whether pitching or using other techniques.

75 "We go to the backs of creeks and the far ends of the coves. The dingy water up the lake usually will heat up faster, and the overall depth of water is shallower. The warmer water, as long as it doesn't exceed 68 degrees, will have a more active bite.

76 "Note that while pitching to the bank can produce males, fishing on the other side of the boat can produce the bigger females. Depending upon the cover and depth, a switch to deeper water might be a better tactic for catching larger females in spring.

77 "Don't hesitate to get as shallow as eight or 12 inches. Nothing is more fun than super-shallow males. The bite is aggressive. If you're in a good area, the action will be non-stop.

"A final note is a bite calls for an immediate hookset when pitching. Don't wait. Bites can be light. When you see any indication of a bite, it's time to set the hook."

Other Seasons

"We do not hesitate pitching anytime we think fish are shallow," says Travis. "Cool or cold water can be good, too, but spring and fall are generally the best times for a weekend fisherman to pitch. Serious winter fishermen should never ignore trying shallow spots. Winter is my favorite time when water temperature is about 42 degrees with fish three to four feet deep."

CORKING

Corking gets high ratings because it's relatively simple to learn and perform, requires little equipment and is deadly when used at the right time.

"Corking is like jigging and pitching— very low cost with a rod/reel and basic tackle being all that's required," says Charles. "It's an easy technique but a little more difficult if the wind is blowing.

"Corking is basically pitching but using a float. A cork is best when the bait needs to be slowed or stopped. Where a freefall pitch technique allows several depths to be fished on each pitch, a cork keeps the bait at one depth where the active fish are located. The float gives precise depth control.

78 "I have trouble slowing down," says Travis. "A float makes me do that. Also, it forces me to leave a bait still instead of jigging, twitching or popping it like I do.

79 "Match the cork to the jig. That's very important. A float that's too big won't lay right and a crappie can feel the resistance. If the float is too small, it will sink or set too low in the water. It's your strike indicator, so you want it to be just right.

"We use a stick type float so when we twitch the float the jig hops up a few inches. It provides a lift, fall, lift, fall motion. I want mine clipped to the line. Dad prefers a slip-float setup.

"A weekend fisherman should keep it easy and simple. Thill makes floats that are matched by weight. Their 1/16-ounce float is made for a 1/16 jig, or, equivalent split-shot with a minnow hook. That makes it easy and exact."

80 Charles comments, "A 9-foot pole is my choice for corking. I use a 9-foot BnM Float & Fly because it gives quicker hooksets. This is important when wind puts a bow in the line. A shorter rod won't let us get rid of the slack and set the hook in one motion. Also, the leverage of the longer rod is good for controlling a crappie coming out of the brush.

"Line is 6-pound-test monofilament for corking. The only time we use braid for corking is when we've been jig fishing and use the same pole. The jigging pole works, but it is longer than necessary.

81 "Travis likes a clip-on float, but I prefer a slip-float. The slip-float forces me to go very slow. If I move it too fast, the line will move up through the float causing the jig to rise too much. So I can only hop it a little. That's good because it makes me work the bait slowly. Also, the slip-float is easier to flip for distance.

82 "A trick I use a lot is shooting the slip-float rig, especially in more open water. Shooting gives me better control than casting. Also, it keeps the bait lower so on windy days the line doesn't catch as much wind.

83 "Wind can make corking more difficult, but don't shy away from a windy bank. A ripple is a huge advantage because the fish are less spooky. It's difficult for them to see you or the boat."

84 Travis says, "We are talking specifically about corking, but I will also cork while jig fishing. The difference is basically just where we are fishing. A cork will let a bait sit still when jigging because I get in too big a hurry. Even when I try to hold a jig still, I can't keep it as still as I can with a float. We use our 12-foot jigging pole and fish just like we would jigging.

85 "A slight rise or twitch of a float is a bite. Set the hook. I fished side by side a guy using the exact same rig in the same spot; he caught one and I caught 24. I told him he had to set the hook when he got a bite. He said his float never went under. If a fisherman waits until a float goes under to set the hook, he has missed the majority of the fish that day."

Springtime Corking

86 "A lot of bites in shallow water are sideways bites," says Travis. "Mainly because the fish can't go down. If the float moves to the side set the hook.

87 "Be sure to keep moving and find the banks holding crappie. There is no use wasting time in areas that don't have fish. Search until you find them. Prespawn is great and so is spawn.

88 "Crappie season is when fish go up in the brush. Take your family and enjoy it. A float is good for young, inexperienced fishermen because it keeps their bait from getting too deep and indicates when a fish has it."

Summer Corking

89 "Corking is corking no matter what season. Corking is good to about 10 feet and then other methods are best, at least for us. But the technique will work anytime the fish are not too deep.

90 "We do a lot of corking in summer. We catch a lot of fish in two feet of water when it's 90 degrees outside. In most lakes, fish will

ERCURY

be deeper. The fishing can be very good during summer if you get in the right depth of water."

91 Charles says, "Rod length is dependent upon how we are corking. We may use a short 7-foot pole, usually a 9-foot, but will switch to a 12-foot Ultralight for straight up and down jigging or pitching."

Winter Corking

Travis says, "Winter is a great time to cork. We do it at Lake of the Ozarks. We'll throw it in open water to schools of fish. The advantage is you can make long casts without getting close and spooking them.

92 "An open-water presentation is a simple twitch, stop, twitch, stop. Do different actions to see what the crappie want. Depths are usually two to five feet deep over deep, open water.

93 "Typical spots at Lake of the Ozarks are Coffin Beach and the main lake 6-mile marker. We usually fish the main lake and the little coves off it. We'll fish brushpiles off docks. On the Gravois Arm, we'll go up in it and do the same thing in front of the docks and shoot the docks.

94 "Winter crappie, in more open water, like to hold in the 12- to 14-foot cover," says Travis. "We will set our corks to get right over the top of it maybe in eight to 10 feet.

95 "This one will be hard for many readers to believe. We'll find a sunlit rocky bank and fish six inches under a float in about a foot to three feet of water. We're talking basic fishing with a cork and float in cold weather. Be sure to at least give try it on your home water.

96 "In a clear-water lake, catch the wind blowing into a bank for a day or two. It will blow algae and pull baitfish into the windblown bank. Crappie and other species will go with the bait. Fishing can be fantastic."

MUDDY WATER
BAITS

CHAPTER 5
SPAWNING & HIGH WATER

SPAWNING

The words "Spawn" and "Crappie" are connected to great spring fishing. Fishermen, who may only go fishing several times a year, always look forward to the spring spawn. It signals the start of fishing season for most weekend fishermen.

97 "The lakes in Missouri get into the upper 50s and 60s sometime in April," says Charles. "Obviously, depending upon where a fisherman lives and his home waters, will determine the dates when water warms to these temperatures. Weather patterns are usually terrible that time of year because of cold fronts. A week of stable weather is good thing, and usually means very good fishing.

98 "Males are moving to the banks making the beds. In stained waters, the males are out four to 12 feet when they are waiting to go in. Then they move shallow. The males go to the bank first and are the shallowest. The fish are aggressive up until they get on the beds, then they will become harder to catch."

99 Charles says, "Any bottom difference, like a chunk rock, pea gravel or any other type, is a good place to try. The pea gravel and sand are just the bottoms crappie like best, so that's what a fisherman needs to look for.

100 "We may be shooting docks, shooting shade or working the banks. We might also be dipping timber located in the same spawning areas.

101 "It may sound funny but we will shoot under overhanging limbs along the bank," says Charles. "That's an excellent way to keep a distance from the fish but get the jig right to them.

102 "All we've been discussing has been fishing with jigs, but minnows will work for some techniques and situations. A buddy and I went to a spawning cove and the water was so clear we were actually sight fishing. One of the first passes through, we were throwing jigs at them. The males would put their noses to the jig and not hit. We went to a minnow hooked through the lips under a float and they did the same thing. We hooked the minnow under the dorsal fin and used no weight with a float. They wouldn't hit the jig or the lip-hooked minnow but would hit the weightless minnow hooked through the back."

HIGH WATER

Few fishermen like the thought of heavy rains and high water. There are periods of good fishing, but there are also many negatives associated with the high waters. The heaviest rains are usually in spring so that's when most of the tips are geared.

SWIFT. SILENT. SECURE.

Stages of High Water

Stage one: "The front and storms are on the way and arrive," says Travis. "A front in spring will push fish into structure, cover and ledges. If the fish are roaming fish, a front will push them tighter to something."

Stage two: "Water comes in and there is a big rise. A lake like Grenada, where the fish are used to the dingy water, it might slow them a little but not stop them. How much mud is being carried into a lake is important. Every lake is different, and finding the best water possible is important. Early in the rise, the best water will likely be the main lake," says Travis.

Stage three: "A few days later, the fishing will be tough but the fish are settling down. I want to go find and fish water that was pushed out ahead of the fresh water. I have seen fish that were holding in beds and cover near the bank before the rain, then the lake rise 10 feet and the fish would still be in the same place, except now they are in water that is 10 feet deeper. Fishing shallow might be good, but many of the fish may still be in their spot where they were before the rise."

Stage four: "Water is falling. Fish move out. The bite can be tough."

High-Water Tips

103 "High water has low oxygen in it," Travis comments. "However, what happens is when the water gets high into the green stuff, like a willow, the green leaves will put oxygen into the water and acts as a filter to make the water cleaner within the tree limbs. Crappie like that situation and will get right in the thick of it. So pay close attention to a bush or tree to see if the water might be a little clearer than the surrounding water. This means a better bite.

"In 2019 we saw so much high water that many waters were still high during summer. The first few weeks after a rise, the fish usually will move to shallower water covers. But after that, the fish may move out into open water where they will suspend and feed on shad during summer. Places like Kentucky Lake have a bottom filled with cover, but the fish may be suspended up in deep water hitting crankbaits or jigs.

104 "The amount of rise required to get into the trees and bushes depends upon growth along the shoreline in previous years. Usually, four or five feet is enough to be a factor. Stable water is critical for the bite to be good.

105 "Falling water in a lake causes fish to pull out, and usually the bite is slow. The rate of water drop is important. A very slow fall isn't bad, but rapid falling water usually means a tougher bite.

106 "Spring is a great time to work shallow waters from transition areas up to shallow bank areas. High water creates an entirely new situation by putting cover at different depths while opening up new covers and previously covered ground."

CHAPTER 6
CRANKBAITS: TROLLING & JERKBAITS

Trolling crankbaits gets a high rating in more open-water lakes during the warm-water months. It's very difficult to learn and perform. The costs are very high.

Charles says, "It's not easy, and it's a lot of work. Costs are expensive from setup to buying and replacing crankbaits."

Travis says, "Planer boards do several things. One, they get baits away from the boat so we aren't spooking as many fish. The pressure from the trolling motor will go six or seven feet down in the water, a big motor 14 or 15 feet, so when you go over these fish they feel that pressure. Blasting that fish with oxygen and pressure, it's easy to see why they often will spook before the crankbait gets to them.

"Two, planer boards give a lot wider trolling path.

"Three, boards allow more versatility in speeds and presentations."

107 "Crankbaits are known as summer troll baits," says Travis. "They've earned that reputation because they produce so well when fish are suspended up in the water column. Spring and fall can be good trolling times, too.

108 "Planer boards actually let you cover a lot more water. Planer boards also let us slow the cranks down more. This means we can vary the speeds down to a much slower than normal speed if we need to.

109 "Use a planer board setup for tighter turns with the boat. With straight lines they will start stacking up on the side of the boat. The planer boards will work their way right around the boat.

110 "Planer boards are great for crankbaits but we also pull jigs with them. We recommend going about 0.5 mile per hour with the jigs. We often parallel banks with jigs when fish are somewhat shallow.

111 "Cranks can be pulled fast, but we like to slow them down more than most. We will get down to 0.8 mile per hour. Run that through a ball of shad, and the crappie will come a little ways to get it. It's important to vary speeds until you learn what they like on that day."

112 Charles says, "Pink and orange are our favorite crankbait colors.

113 "You need equipment capable of handling a planer board and a fish. We use a BnM Catfish pole. Our boards are by Off-Shore Tackle.

114 "Use sinkers to get baits down without using too much line. The Shad Pole is a sinker-downrigger item that angles into the water. The weight pulls it down, and so does the water pressure against it. It's a good way for a fisherman to get depth out of almost any crankbait.

115 "Use crankbaits in fall before the fish go shallow. Some fish will go very shallow. Others will transition to mainly open-water areas like ledges, points and big flats. Sometimes a crankbait will work in early fall because it covers a lot of water.

116 "Line size should be small in diameter so you can keep the baits down but strong enough to pull you free from some of the hangups. Also, you'll catch large catfish and other stuff that's easier with a heavier line. We use 12-pound-test line."

JERKBAIT ... WINTER CASTING

Action is unbelievable when you hit it right. Travis loves the method, saying people have no idea how good a crankbait can be in winter. If you can stand the cold and are on the right body of water, the big, long jerkbait-style crankbaits are deadly for catching crappie.

Charles hates the method. He doesn't like jerking a bait five times and then waiting two minutes, jerking again, and waiting another two minutes.

Equipment can be a good bass rod and some quality baits.

The time is winter and it's for deep, clear lakes.

117 "Watch the water temperatures," says Travis. "When the temperatures hit the low 40s it starts getting good.

118 "Look for the shallow, mid-depth fish. In general, fish will be in the 10- to 12-foot range on our home lake, Ozark. The fish will come up to hit a crank at five feet deep. Other lakes may be different.

119 "Throw a 2.5- to 5.5-inch jerkbait on 8-pound fluorocarbon line. I prefer a 6-foot-long ultra-stiff pole.

120 "Try different retrieves. A big jerkbait needs an erratic action. Maybe a jerk, jerk, stop. The jerkbait will sit suspended in the water. It sits dead still. When you jerk it hard it will turn around and look the other direction and turn back again. It goes from dead still to an erratic motion and the fish can't stand it.

121 "It's a fun and challenging way to fish because you never know which way the school of fish are going to go. When you have several schools in one area, it's best to go from school to school. It's the best way to find the most active and biggest fish.

122 "If you run over a school of predator fish and scatter them, you can catch them with a crankbait.

123 "Target brushpiles. Crappie will be in open water, but they'll also hold in or over brushpiles. A 4.5-inch jerkbait is very good for pulling the crappie out to hit.

124 "Don't look for the pretty, round balls of bait. Don't fish these because it's a waste of time. These shad are doing their natural thing of swimming around in that tight ball. When you see shad are stringy looking and you see fish underneath them, it's exactly what you want. They look that way because the fish are feeding on the baitfish.

125 "We are talking jerkbaits, but you can usually do the same thing with a jig and float. You don't have to do anything fancy with the jig. Just cast it out and reel it back. You can count it down to get to the right depth. Or, use a float to keep it at the right depth and fish it slow."

126 Which jerkbait? "How much money do you want to spend? Rogue baits come in a wide variety of prices. A Lucky Craft DD70 is good."

The summary? Look for schools of baitfish that are no deeper than eight feet over deep water. Cast to them and stay with the school. If you don't like the big jerkbaits, use a jig and float.

BALZOUT

CHAPTER 7
SLOW TROLLING ... TECHNIQUE, ROADBEDS, FACTORS & TOURNAMENT TIPS

Slow trolling, called spider rigging by some, gets the highest overall rating as a year-round, versatile, any-water technique. It's start-up costs are high because it requires electronics, pole-holder racks and multiple long poles. However, when the setup is completed, costs are no more than for any other technique.

The misconception is that a fisherman can put poles out, lean back in the seat and relax, but there's much more to it than that. The technique starts with finding the right spot, rigging and baiting. The presentation includes total boat control, watching electronics, avoiding hangups but keeping baits in cover, keeping fresh bait on and watching closely for bites. Occasionally there will be a massive re-rigging required when a school of white bass tangles every hook. This tactic is a lot of work.

Another problem is the name of the technique. Spider rigging, slow trolling, and trolling are a few common ones. Slow trolling is the most accurate because the poles are placed in close proximity on the front of the boat so all of them are in the same brushpile or on the same ledge.

The spider rigging name came from having poles placed all around the boat making the boat look like a spider with long legs.

It still works today but placing poles where all baits are in the strike zone is better.

THE TECHNIQUE

The technique includes fishermen side-by-side on the front deck. Speeds range from stopped to about 0.6 mile per hour. Average is 0.3 mile per hour with a fisherman stopping at a good brushpile or other potential spot. The fishermen help each other with electronics, bites, netting fish and handling poles. If a fisherman has to get up, the other fishermen has all duties until the partner returns. An inexperienced fisherman can use two poles while an experienced fisherman may use eight where legal. The normal setup is four poles per experienced fisherman.

127 "Speeds are 0.0 to 0.5 miles per hour," says Charles. "A slow presentation usually gets the bigger bite.

128 "Occasionally, we will go with the wind if the wind is strong. Power Poles or chains are popular ways to slow or stop the boat.

129 "We usually go against the wind. Boat control is critical and going into the wind allows the best control.

130 "Do not be afraid to put baits into the brush. We might have to tie 100 times a day, but that's part of it. Fishing the spot should be done as slowly as possible. However, when going from spot to spot, go fast.

131 "Attack a new lake by trying as many depths as possible," says Charles. "We try different techniques, too. Trolling is just one method, but it's a very important one.

132 "Electronics are important. We couldn't do it without them. Probably 90 percent of our scouting is with our electronics. A fisherman should look to see if fish are suspended, grouped, tight to cover, under docks or whatever. We spend a lot of time in the areas where the bigger fish should be located.

133 "We use a lot of minnows when slow trolling. Straight minnows work but so do jigs tipped with minnows. Plastic is easier to use and catches a lot of bigger fish, but plastic is the worst at being good one time and not the next. I'm not sure why.

134 "Equipment consistency is very important for the weekend fishermen who slow trolls," says Charlie. "It doesn't matter if it's a 12-foot Ozark or 16-foot BnM pole, every pole needs to be identical. The reason is, when you and a partner have six or eight poles out, everything must look the same. The pole tips are bent equally so when one is out of place it means there is a fish on.

135 "Line size should be the same on all trolling poles. Line diameter causes water drag when going through the water so, if it's not the same, some lines will be at different angles and the pole tips will have different pull on them. We use 12-pound high-vis main line and 8-pound-test leaders.

136 "Bait rig weight should be the same," continues Charles. "Again, it's a matter of every pole tip looking the same. If pole tips are identical, bites will look exactly the same on each pole. There is no guessing.

137 "Bait rigs can be tied to the main line as needed or rigs can be pre-tied. We pre-tie because it is much quicker to do on the water, and we put baits into the cover so we lose a lot.

138 "A weekend fisherman might prefer a T-bar and pole holders to keep things simple. Individual Capps/Coleman pole holders, one for each rod, are better but expensive. They allow maximum adjustment and separate poles so bites do not affect other poles.

139 "When adjusting poles in holders, get all the rod tips the same distance from the water and the separation between poles the same. That way it's easy to see when one is out of place. One out of place means a bite or the rig is against cover. Because partners often watch each other's poles, it's critical all poles be the same. I hate to repeat that, but it's very important, and we see that problem a lot when watching other fishermen.

140 "Put baits into the cover as much as possible. A weekend fishermen don't like this because it's too much work changing rigs during the day. That's up to the fisherman. Travis and I are serious about catching fish so we will do whatever it takes to catch more and bigger fish.

141 "The worst situations for us are when gar and white bass tangle every rig. It's time to get them all in and re-rig.

142 "Slow trolling isn't for every situation. Clear water isn't easy to troll so we try to stay out of it if it is too clear."

Fall Slow Trolling

143 "The water is starting to get cooler so the fish will start chasing the balls of shad," says Charles. "You can follow the shad and usually find and catch crappie.

144 "I believe 90 percent of the time, the slower you go the more chance for a big fish bite. Big crappie didn't get big by being overly aggressive.

145 "Jigs are good when slow trolling. Colors are important. Orange glow is one of my favorites on Grenada. Black-chartreuse is another good color in most lakes.

146 "Use jigs with big hooks. It's important. We like a 2/0 or 3/0 hook because we lose fewer fish. Our jighead is a Muddy Water Whack'em.

147 "You have to keep baits down even when moving faster. We will switch from a ½-ounce to a 1½-ounce sinker."

Winter Slow Trolling

"We do use a lot of techniques," says Charles, "but slow trolling is a major part of our fishing. There are times we will push baits to crappie other fisherman might jig or cast to but never slow troll. Trolling in thick cover is a matter of getting more baits down in the water to improve our odds.

148 "Any season, including winter, can be a good time to slow troll. Winter is a time to find the schools of shad. The balls show up on electronics, especially if you have a Side Imaging unit, but any electronics will work. We mark them and then try to mark more nearby. Then we put our poles down and work those schools.

149 "Water is 40 degrees or colder in winter here in the Ozarks. Your lake may be different. The lake we fish has clear water so the shad will likely be eight to 12 feet but could be much shallower, over water that's 20 feet and deeper. The crappie are just below the shad no matter the overall depth of the water. Follow the school of shad.

150 "The biggest factor for clear, winter water is to have some wind. A ripple on the water makes the fish less spooky. If water is smooth and clear, it's best to cast.

151 "Stay warm. You can't fish if you're freezing. Dress in layers. Wear a mask. We carry 10 pairs of inexpensive jersey gloves and change them often when they get wet."

ROADBEDS & FACTORS

Roadbeds aren't everywhere, but the Buntings look for them on the lakes where they travel. Most contour maps show where the old roads were located when the lake was built. Electronic maps are more up to date but include most of the old stuff, too.

Roadbeds can be good all year long. The key is going to the right depth and being in an area that holds fish. Crappie use the roads and associated contours with because they provide "something different" where they can travel and hold.

152 "Look for a hard bottom when looking for roadbeds. It may have silt over the top, but the bottom will be harder than the surrounding area," says Charles.

153 "Watch electronics for rocks, ditches and trees. If surrounding fields were cleared by farmers, they had to move the rocks to the edges and that was sometimes along the roads. Trees usually grew up along the edges of the roads for windbreaks or because of fence lines. The edges of the road can be excellent.

154 "Trees can be jigged, but some areas can be slow trolled. Our rigs are the typical Capps/Coleman double-hook style, but we always have a jig on the bottom. Above that an egg weight and above that a leader and minnow hook.

155 "If you catch more fish on the jig tipped with a minnow, try sliding a solid soft plastic body on the shank of your minnow hook, then tip with a minnow.

156 "Speed is very important when trolling a roadbed. Don't skip any area because a lot of our bites come in open water where we don't expect them. The speed is important, and sometimes sitting still is best. You'll have to try different speeds but start slow."

157 Travis says, "Like with any technique, today's electronics can be a big advantage. It lets a fisherman know where the fish are located and what, if anything, they are relating to. It's important to remember that some spots may not have fish on them in the morning, but will be covered up later in the day when the sun is at a different angle."

FACTORS

158 "Strong wind can be a problem," says Travis. "We have a big glass boat that allows us to fish in the wind and still have boat control. But a recreational fisherman doesn't have to stay out in the wind. Don't fish those windy areas when there are protected coves and creeks to get in.

"The velocity of the wind is the key issue. A fisherman must be able to maintain full control of the boat while catching fish, watching the graph, baiting hooks and turning to toss a fish in the livewell. So, if you can safely fish and maintain control of the boat and baits, it's probably not too windy. If it's too strong, find a protected area.

"Wind is not always the enemy. In winter, the wind often dictates where the fish will be located. When the wind isn't too strong, but has been blowing consistently into a bank, fish will stack up there. Casting might work better, but it's important to pay attention to wind.

"Most people think having no wind is an ideal situation, but it's not. It's terrible for slow trolling. Fish are spooky and can see the boat. Boat control becomes a problem because we slow troll into the wind so when we let off the trolling motor, the boat will stop and move backwards. This keeps us from running over the top of fish and spooking them. Also, if we catch a fish or get hung up, the boat backs us away from the cover."

Charles says, "A light or no-wind tactic is using corks while slow-trolling.

Corks will show light bites you may not see on your pole tip.

159 "Cold fronts in spring can cause fish to go down, get tight to cover, or both. That could force you to switch to jigging to get the bait down into the trees and cover."

160 Charles doesn't like current so tries to avoid it. Travis says, "On a river, how fast it rises or falls changes the speed of the current. Also, a falling river can create eddies where a point becomes so shallow it creates a current break and fish will stack up behind it. When current swings around and creates an eddy, it's a good place to fish. Lakes can have current, too, due to wind or releasing water."

161 Charles says, "Fishing pressure can be a problem, particularly in spring. A well-known area can be pressured all year long, but in general, spring is usually worse. If an area is pressured, it's important to slow down."

162 Pleasure boaters and jet skis can be a problem. Travis says, "When the pleasure boat traffic is heavy, the first thing crappie do is go deeper. They will go down and maybe shut off. Fishermen who are already fishing in 20 feet or deeper may be okay, but boat control can be a problem with too many waves.

"The worse wave action is the sideways action caused by boat waves. They can come from all different directions so control is difficult. Even if fishing something like a dock, waves can crash your boat into the dock. There is nothing fun about fishing in pleasure-boat traffic."

163 Travis continues, "Rising and falling water can be good or bad. We won the Classic at Tombigbee with the river on a fast fall. We fished spots on day one that were on the bank on day two. That's a fast fall, but we were catching fish.

164 "Low water has advantages. The water has the same number of fish but much less water so the fish are congregated. Another advantage is more structure sticking out of the water. Even with today's electronics, it's easier to fish something that's sticking out of the water than something you can't see. You get to fish structure you haven't fished all year long and learn cover that will be good when the water comes back up.

"Winter is the obvious time when water gets low. Flood-control lakes are pulled down starting in fall or early winter and are kept low until spring.

"Summer waters can get low, too. Pull downs, lack of rain and evaporation can create low water. It's a good time to catch fish.

165 "Sun and clouds can be good or bad," Travis continues. "I can't predict which will be best but I prefer the sun. Fish don't like bright light penetration so the sun moves them to cover or other shade. If light is not a problem, they can roam around and will be less likely to be at the cover I drop my bait into. On a muddy lake during warm seasons, sun or clouds usually doesn't matter.

"Some covers will be better at different times of day. A ledge or cover may provide shade at certain times and be stacked with fish, while other times fish will be gone. Being at the right place at the right time is critical. We see it on many of the lakes we go to and especially on our home lake we often fish. I don't like the cloudy days because fish can be scattered, but they will bite in either situation.

"Jig color depends upon water color. For example, Grenada in spring is muddy so orange glow, pink-lemon glow and Outlaw green-chartreuse are good colors. They usually won't catch a crappie in clear water on a bright day because fish want a more natural bait like blue ice. But let the clear lake get cloudy or stained just a little, then the brighter bold colors will work. And colors can change throughout the day so don't hesitate to switch and try different colors.

166 "We fished clear water in a tournament at Stockton Lake in Missouri a several years ago. We seldom fish deeper than 12 feet anywhere we go, but the shallowest we could fish there was 15 feet deep, but most of the fish were deeper because the water was so clear. We went as far upriver as we could go until we finally found some slightly stained water. We caught shallower fish.

167 "I like 12 to 18 inches of visibility in the water. I think the fish will be shallower where we like to fish. If fishing in 30 feet of water, there is a big water column to search. It can take forever for a jig to get down to 25 feet. But in six feet of water, I can find crappie quicker because I know they will be near bottom. I've got a better strike zone and can get a jig in it quickly. I can cover more water and fish more cover."

168 "Water temperatures? Every fisherman loves spring. The water temperature I like for white crappie is about 58 to 60 degrees. That's big fish time because the females are full of eggs.

169 Summer temperatures? "In summer the water is hot. I don't care about the temperature because it will either be hot or hotter, it doesn't matter. Lakes with cover can have crappie positioned shallow. In more open lakes, the fish will be in open water above the thermocline, chasing shad or just suspended. Shad are often near the surface because the oxygen levels are better. Shallow lakes really have shallow thermoclines so pay attention. The fish will be above it."

170 Fall temperatures? "Fall can be a tricky time. It's difficult to fish in 70- to 80-degree water because fish are transitioning and moving all the time. That's usually the time of crappie classic tournaments, and it's often our most difficult tournament of the year because fish are hard to pattern.

"Water hitting temperatures in the 60s in fall changes everything. I can fish almost like in springtime and in the same areas. Fishing can be really good."

171 Travis says, "Winter is when I throw hard, bass-type jerkbaits out in open water in clear lakes. I find the shad then throw a suspending jerkbait. It's slow but deadly. We can also catch them in shallow water with a cork and jig. If a fisherman is catching fish to eat, deep water offers a lot of action in winter. A friend of mine caught a bunch of fish last winter at 50 feet deep."

"Barometric pressure can make a big difference, but I don't pay attention to it because I work most of the time and have to go fishing when I can go fishing. That's usually tournament days, so I'm going fishing no matter what the barometer is doing.

172 "The perfect day to fish? I want to fish in spring with the water temperature at 60 degrees. I like the air to be warm because I want to be comfortable. The sun needs to be out because it positions the fish. I want a consistent weather pattern for five days. Wind will be five to 10 miles per hour. And the fish are biting. That's the day I'll catch my biggest fish of the year."

TOURNAMENT TIPS

173 "The key to doing good in tournaments is to learn a pattern," says Charles. "Slow trolling helps because more baits increase the odds of catching fish to learn the pattern.

174 "Electronics gives information. Don't skip on this step. Take your time looking and watching. The time spent using electronics will lead to more fish.

175 "When we catch a couple of fish, we pay attention to get as much information as possible from those fish. What was the bottom depth? What was the depth of the fish? What speed were we moving? What bait and color? Was the bottom sloping? What type of cover? The key is to repeat what works so pay attention to each fish you catch," says Charles.

176 "We've mentioned this several times, but noting what areas are good during different times of the day is an important tip. We've learned that some spots might be best in early morning, or 10:00 in the morning or at 2:00 in the afternoon. Test good-looking spots at different times during the day to see if fish are active.

177 "If we have good information that an area holds 3-pound fish and we catch a 1.75 and 2.0 while prefishing, you won't see us there again. We've marked it and will be back tournament day. Tournament fishermen should not keep fishing and catching fish from areas where they will be on tournament day. A recreational fisherman can stay there and catch fish.

178 "Sometimes fish want something different. For example, in a tournament in Mississippi, we had to push 1.5-ounce weights at a fast speed to catch fish that were suspended up one to two feet under the surface. We were catching fish very shallow just under the surface. The fish wanted baits to be fast if they were going to hit them. It was a reaction bite. Sometimes a fisherman has to try something different.

179 "There are times we slow troll where some fishermen jig. We might just use three poles each, but we put them into the brush.

It's hard work, but we can often catch more fish. It's a great tournament tactic but good for weekend fishermen, too. To practice this, try two poles. Have pre-tied rigs ready or at least what you need for tying rigs because you'll lose some. Putting poles into the brush is a mental thing, knowing you will get hung up but improving your odds of catching fish can be worth it."

BALZOUT
Tite-Lok
MO 1439 GA
SECURE.

CHAPTER 8
RUN & GUN SLOW TROLLING

"We've always tried to do our own thing," says Travis, "not just copy what other fishermen are doing. When we go to a lake, we like to try every technique to see which ones work best. Matching a technique to the cover and area is usually best. Spider rigging often wins as our best technique.

"To discuss further on doing our own style of fishing, it makes sense for improving our odds in the tournaments. For example, if I go into a creek where Cory Batterson is pulling crankbaits and I pull crankbaits too, he will win. He is an expert at it. I might go somewhere else and find bigger fish, but I won't beat him at his game in his area. The same if 10 of the best slow trollers are in an area I want to fish. My odds are not good of beating all of them. So we look for our own style of fishing and look hard to find areas where we don't see a lot of other boats.

"Run-and-gun slow trolling is just a combination of things we've learned," continues Travis. "We were lucky to put it together early before others were doing it. When we were successful using it, others quickly adopted the style.

"We like to teach others how to catch fish, but when the run-gun trolling had such good success, fishermen wouldn't leave us alone. They were trying to figure out what we were doing, and it got so bad we couldn't even sort our fish at a tournament because so many were asking questions and looking at the stuff in our boat. We started pulling into other parking lots, sorting our fish and then go to the weigh-in parking lot."

180 Travis discusses their go-to technique. "Run-and-gun slow trolling is just about the math. For a weekend fisherman, it might be fishing 20 beds instead of 10. For our tournament fishing, it's fishing as many beds as possible. If we work hard and fish 40 beds in a day vertical jigging, that is good. If we line up 20 beds in that same area in a fence-row-type pattern that we can fish slow trolling, and say I make 20 moves that day, that's 240 beds. And that's times 16 hooks. Mathematically, most fishermen can't keep up.

"Run-and-gun means taking enough time at a spot to catch the fish, but going fast to the next spot. Don't fish between the spots and waste time.

181 "If you place beds, put them where they can be fished efficiently. This allows more fish from one area without moving a lot.

182 "One trick we've done is drop beds in a row, but stagger them so one is on one side of the boat and the next one on the other side of the boat. If Dad's poles are in a bed, it allows me to bait or adjust my poles, but I'm always ready to net a fish if he hangs a good one. I'll be fishing the next bed while he is rigging and ready to net. It's a good way to fish efficiently.

183 "If you want to use this tactic, work on hitting as many spots as possible during the day. It's okay to go back and hit spots again if they are really good or have a history of big fish.

184 "For us, depending upon how far apart our spots are located, we like to move 38 to 45 times a day. That's eight poles up and eight poles down. But it's quicker than jigging because you can fish a bed many times quicker with 16 baits slow trolling than jigging with one bait.

185 "Baits are a concern. Minnows are a pain, but they add action to a pole that is stuck in a rod holder. A bigger minnow gives a bigger profile and scent. A smaller minnow is quicker and puts off more vibrations.

186 "No matter what style of slow trolling a fisherman choses, sensitive rod tips are critical. If a pole is too stiff, you won't see as many bites. A soft tip reveals what's happening below at the bait. Tournament fishermen have learned that 16-foot poles with sensitive tips will help catch more fish.

187 "Keep your hands on the pole racks or holders. You can feel bites you may not see. Also, if you are looking away you still feel the bite.

"To summarize run-gun slow trolling, it's targeting specific targets and not just fishing open water. Down south, fishermen put their hooks in the water and take off trolling. Run-gun means not wasting time fishing between beds or cover."

SLOW TROLLING EQUIPMENT

Some tackle and equipment has been previously discussed, but here is a summary of the Buntings' slow trolling equipment:

Poles: 16-foot BGJP BnM jigging poles; or 12-foot BnM Ultra-Lites.

Line: Vicious 12-pound-test high-visibility main line; 8-pound-test leaders.

Baits: Double-rigs, Capps/Coleman style with egg sinker between the baits. Bottom bait is usually a ⅛-ounce jig tipped with a minnow. Next up the line is a ⅜-ounce egg sinker (¼ to 1.5-ounces). Above the sinker about 12 to 24 inches is a leader with a minnow hook. The bait can be a straight minnow. or the hook can have a plastic body on the shank above the minnow.

"Since this book started about three years ago," says Charles, "we have probably changed our rigs five times, making small adjustments. The basic rig we've described is a good one. However, this year (2019) we are eliminating all the hardware because we stick our rigs in the brush and cover so anything that might catch on something results in more hangups.

"The new rig is difficult to explain, but in the brush we'll likely keep it short so we'll start with about a 30-inch, 8-pound-test piece of line. We'll double it, leaving one side longer than the other. We grab it where it's doubled and run it around itself three times and then through the loop to form a loop knot with about a 1-inch loop.

"On the bottom of the rig, I'll likely put a 5⁄16 Whack'em Jig about 14 inches down from the loop. I'll tie it with a Palomar knot. Trim. On the other tag end, I'll tie a Palomar knot on a minnow hook as close to the leader loop as possible, creating about a 1.5-inch leader. The minnow on top has a little room to swim but not too much to get hung up in limbs. If I'm catching a fish and the other leader gets hung up, it breaks at the loop so I don't lose the fish. I tie the main line to the rig with a clinch knot. If in open water and not in the brush, I'll separate everything a lot more. An egg sinker can go between the jig and loop knot when needed."

Pole holders: Driftmaster singles with full adjustment.

Trolling motor: Minn Kota Ultrex

CHAPTER 9
JIGHEADS, SCENTS & SPINNERS

Every fisherman has his or her preference for a jig. The jig consists of a head and body. Jighead factors include the head color, weight, barb and hook size. Therefore, a jighead plays an important role.

JIGHEADS

188 "When slow trolling," says Charles, "we've mentioned that a 1/8-, 5/16- or 1/4-ounce jighead works great on the bottom of the rig. The egg sinker on the rig is often 3/8-ounce but is determined by depth of water and boat speed.

189 "Shooting docks, I typically use a 1/32-ounce while Travis uses a 1/16-ounce. Two weights give different presentations. I'll also use bigger plastic to slow the fall even more. The 1/16-ounce is also good for corking.

190 "Hook size is very important. A #1 is the minimum size we use because we are going after big fish, but all but the tiny fish will eat it, too. I pour my own and had to modify the mold for the hooks to fit. Now we are using Whack'em jigs because they have big hooks.

191 "Dipping in the trees, I'll use a ⅛-ounce a lot," Charles continues. "The heavier jig provides better placement and control of the bait. The control of the fall can be controlled by using your off hand to pull and release line. I'll drop it a little, stop it, drop a little and then jig it. I'll go all the way to the bottom and work back up.

192 "Use a ¼-ounce jig when jigging aggressive crappie. If fish are there in 8 feet, 10 or deeper, the jig gets there quickly. It will go through cover and brush better because of the weight. It's good in the wind. A heavier jig also gives better feel.

193 "Never add a split-shot above a jig. The sensitivity is reduced. You can't bump the jig loose with your pole."

195 Travis says, "Colors can vary from lake to lake, but our preference is an orange head, and it works in stained or clear water. Painted eyes look nice, but I don't believe it's important to a crappie.

196 "The hook gap can be a problem when using smaller hooks in a jighead. Years ago, the standard was a #4 hook with a Southern Pro 1.5-inch tube. We use to get bites but not catch the fish. I talked to a bass pro about it, and he said our only option was to use a bigger hook. Today we use a 2/0 or 3/0 in all of our jigs we make. It gives a bigger hook gap. We lose fewer fish now."

SCENTS

Call it scent, attractant, smell-good or magic potion. It makes a jig smell better. A liquid, granular, spray, paste or gel can help you catch more crappie. Some jigs bodies have scent impregnated when poured.

The most popular attractant for crappie is Crappie Nibbles. They have been used for a few decades. Berkley added sparkle to them in 2000 after Larry McMullin hand rolled glitter into his Nibbles, and he and partner Dan Hudgens won the 1999 Crappie USA Classic. Making them was a mess because he rolled regular Nibble in glitter, so the kitchen floor, table and counters didn't impress his wife.

The debate goes on about whether to use a scent with a crappie bait. From hundreds of interviews, I can honestly say that a small percentage of jig fishermen say it's not necessary because they catch fish anyway. However, 80-90 percent of experts believe it is critical when the bite is tough. Many believe it helps catch fish all the time so they always use it. One of the most conclusive arguments is after fishing a spot and crappie quit biting, put scent on a jig to see if you get any more bites. The bottom line is that it doesn't hurt, it can help, so why not use it?

197 "Use scent," says Travis. "Muddy Water baits have scent impregnated in the plastic. I believe in the scent, and having it in the plastic, means it's there all the time. I'll also spray my jigs with garlic-scent spray. It is a nasty spray in the boat, but it works.

198 "Other smells work, but I like garlic because it is something different. They don't smell it all day like they do shad or minnow scent. Why would I want a smell that fish smell all day long? Like if somebody on the couch farts, everyone in the room is looking around wanting to know what and who. Garlic is different so a fish is drawn to the bait to check it out. Another comparison is the black-chartreuse jig that has been good for years and will outfish most others. Fish hit it because they can see it, not because it's the color of something they are feeding on. So garlic has been my choice, and we've had good luck with it. For me it's simple. I'm using a plastic body that has garlic scent, and I'm adding more garlic scent to bring attention to my bait."

Charles says, "We use Bang Garlic Spray Scent. It's a long story, but we weren't catching fish on the second day of a tournament that we were leading. I pulled out the spray and sprayed it on my minnows. Travis said we were using minnows and didn't need the spray. I caught a 2.85 and another good crappie right after spraying. He decided it wasn't a bad idea. We both used it on our minnows and started catching fish."

199 "We've used scent to get rid of odors on our hands. Remember that human scent, gas, oil, coffee, suntan lotion and other odors are bad."

SPINNERS

200 "Try a willow-leaf blade'" says Charles. "We like the willow-leaf when vertical jigging because it gives more flitter-flotter as it falls. Dropping slowly, you get a better reaction strike, especially with the added flash of the willow-leaf blade.

201 "Match the blade color to the water. A copper blade in dark or dingy water is best for maximum visibility and more bites. A silver in clearer water works good.

202 "Pick your blade size. We use a Pro Series Road Runner. Blade size can be important. We use a small blade in warm water and up to a #3 blade in spring and fall. We don't use blades in winter.

203 "A good tactic is for one partner to use a jig with a blade and the other partner not. The purpose is to see what the fish prefer. This is good when the bite is very slow to try to find something they like. Not only that, if I'm fishing behind Travis while jigging

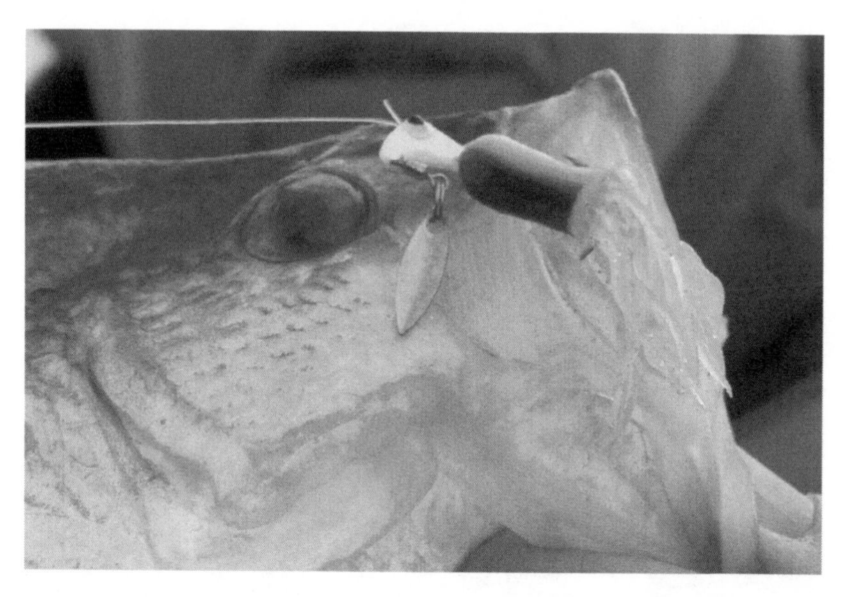

trees, I'm not going to catch fish on the same bait he is using. I've got to use something different," says Charles.

204 Travis recommends a lightweight jig with spinner. "You've heard me say big bait for big fish, but in summer, we've learned that a lot of time a smaller bait fished slower will catch more big crappie. Fish can be sluggish in hot water. By going to a 1/32-ounce jig with a spinner, it'll slow the fall so it drifts down slower.

205 "A blade gives the fish something different and a bigger profile and a little flash. We do use them, but overall, blades are used a small percentage in our fishing.

206 "A jigging trick used by Kevin Rogers and a few others is to put the blade on the line above the jig. It adds flash along with a click when the blade hits the jig eyelet. Again, it's something different for the fish to see and hear and can sometimes give the fisherman a little edge to catch more fish."

CHAPTER 10
FALL TRANSITION & LEDGES

FALL TRANSITION

"Fall transition. It means patterns are changing," says Travis. "Transition in fall is crappie moving from open water to structure. Like here at Truman most will move to hedge trees. In many lakes, it means moving back to stumps or other cover. Water temperatures from 80 to 70 degrees can be a tough period. When the temperatures get below 70 degrees the action picks up.

207 "Fall is the time for fish to go to the cover. That's great because it puts fish on a specific spot.

208 "Keep moving in fall. When you find the fish, you can slow down, but because fish are on the move, keep moving until you find them. Cover as many spots as you can during the day, including ledges at different depths. Move often and hit many spots."

209 Travis says, "A place like Kentucky Lake can be excellent in fall. It's got tons of structure on bottom, and there will always be some fish on it. Before the transition, the fish can be scattered in open water.

210 "You can search spring spawning areas in fall. Crappie will be in the same spots surfing around for shad. Still, the fish will be on cover when possible.

211 "Spider rig in fall. We catch most of our bigger fish on jigs, but we usually tip our jigs with minnows."

Drops & Ledges in Fall

Charles says, "We fish a lot of ledges during the year. Some are small ones on flats and some are the typical drop-offs. We don't fish deep drops like many fishermen do during summer and winter. Therefore, even when fishing for fun, we don't go deep. If someone is just wanting fish to eat, they can catch them deep and put them straight on ice.

"A drop can be good year-round. You just have to find a drop at the depth the fish are using no matter what season you're fishing. In fall, the shallow and mid-depth spots should be perfect."

212 Travis says, "Crappie may be moving around, but some will stay close to a ledge. The fish will use the ledge for reference, but they will be chasing the balls of shad that are also running the ledge. Crappie feed on shad all year long, but in fall they really go after them when the water cools down a little. Find the right ledge and have a lot of fun.

213 "To a crappie, a piece of cover along a ledge is like a pit stop on a highway to us. The fish will run the ledges, see the brush and sink down in it to hide from predators and to ambush baitfish. Around 60 degrees seems to be peak time.

214 "Fall has advantages. One is less fishing pressure. People are hunting so fewer boats are on the lakes," says Travis. "It's just a great time of year to be outdoors and for catching crappie.

215 "The exact depth of crappie is difficult to predict because it changes a lot with the shad. Water temperature and sunlight penetration play a role, but each day can be different. I like to fish points because there are several depths involved, along a drop-off, so chances are good for finding fish at some depth along the drop or up on the flat next to the ledge.

216 "Wind helps in fall because it pushes fish shallower. Look in the coves and creeks where wind is blowing into. Fish will be on shallow ledges.

217 "Like with fishing for any species, be sure to play close attention to your electronics when fishing fall ledges. It will lead you to the best fishing spots. Also look for a bend, change in bottom hardness and cover along the ledge.

218 "Pay attention to very small ledges. I figure if a crappie can put his belly in the mud and his eyes are below the ledge, he will be content.

"Even though fishing pressure is usually less in fall, when the word gets out of great fishing, there will be fishing pressure. This makes tiny drops more important.

"We were in Oklahoma fishing a tournament when this happened. We probably caught 250 off a tiny ledge on a flat. Boats came in all over us but never figured it out. One guy actually came up and asked us how we were catching so many fish. I felt really bad, but because we were in the middle of fishing a tournament, I didn't want to reveal it, so I just told him I guess the fish were just following along with our boat. After the tournament, I would have told him exactly what we were doing if I had seen him.

219 "Pay attention to sun direction. Sun shining from behind a ledge is better because the ledge will create a shadow. Crappie like the shadows. This becomes more important in shallow water."

CHAPTER 11
DOCK PATTERNS & SHOOTING

SHOOTING

Shooting open areas and open docks isn't difficult. Fewer obstacles means an easier shot. However, the best shooting spots are often in tight places with obstacles.

A six-inch gap in floatation with a sweet spot about five feet beyond the opening, presents a challenge. A good shooter can do that and more. The key is practice and lots of it.

Docks have always been prime targets for catching crappie. Some lakes have docks and others don't. Lakes with docks offer year-round opportunities, with summer being a key time, when crappie need shade. But, other seasons can be good, too.

Because boat traffic on Lake of the Ozarks is intolerable during summer, Charles and Travis restrict their dock fishing to fall and winter.

220 Travis says, "A lot of times the fish will move up into four to six feet of water in fall. The temperatures drop and they'll get into the shallows, almost like it's a fake spawn. On lakes with docks, they'll be up under them, and, in lakes without docks, they'll be in cover.

221 "Try shooting docks. Poles should be five to seven feet long. Most fishermen prefer a short pole, but I like a 6 or 6.5-foot Richard Williams BnM, or sometimes a 7-foot rod, rigged with an Abu-Garcia reel. I like a wide-mouth spool because the line comes off easier and smoother, more distance and accuracy. Dad likes the new 6-foot BnM Dock Shooter.

222 "The further back you get the jig, the more and bigger fish you'll catch.

223 "Use high-vis, 6-pound-test line. Vicious high-vis Panfish series is good. We like this line because it's easy to see. When the bait is falling, we'll often see a bite that we can't feel.

224 "Use a jig with a slow fall. We like a 1/32- or 1/16-ounce head. A bigger body bait also helps slow the fall speed. The key on jig weight is to have the right weight for the depth, wind and strike-zone depth.

"Also find the best color for the water you fish. On Ozarks where we fish, the Popsicle, a pink-chartreuse color, is one of the best.

225 "Shooting is definitely the best dock tactic. Shooting gives you so much more accuracy and lets you get into spots you can't get by casting or flipping. The bow-and-arrow technique has been around for a long time, but gets more popular every year.

"My first shot I start reeling as soon as the jig hits. The second shot I count to three. Third shot I might flip the bail, let it sink then work it back to me. If I do it right, I'll learn the strike zone after several shots.

226 "Fishing pressure is a major issue with docks and makes a big difference. Fishing pressure means smaller and fewer fish. The best docks will likely have other fishermen on them.

227 "Try to stay out of boat traffic as much as possible. The dock is going up and down. Fish don't like an unstable dock.

228 "Pick your docks with the wind in mind. Wind can be a boat-control problem. The back of the boat is usually the hardest to control. It can be impossible for one person to control the boat. Bad wind means you have a partner with one shooting and one controlling the boat. It's better to move to an area with less wind.

229 "Learn your docks. There are docks we fish that are more consistent at holding crappie most of the year. It's possible to pull up to a dock and have your limit in 20 minutes. We've learned through the years which docks are good.

230 "Side Imaging is a way to find fish faster in open water, but it is great to have if you are shooting docks. You can idle by a dock and look under it before deciding to fish it.

231 "Clear-water lakes are best for dock fishing. The fish need shade, and they can see the bait a long way," says Travis.

232 "Just because it's spring, you don't need to ignore a dock. The dock's shade becomes more important each day as the sun keeps getting higher.

233 "Check the water temperature. Temperatures ranging from 40 to 70 degrees are good in fall and winter, even spring. Below 40 degrees, the fish tend to chase shad more out in open water.

234 "Use the right jig. One of our dock baits is a Southern Pro Walleye tube, a 2.5-inch bait. By shoving the head back up into the tube, it doesn't tear as easily, and it skips better. More recently, I've got my own Muddy Water Bait that was made for skipping docks. The skips allow a bait to be shot much further back.

235 Travis continues, "It's important for a fisherman to realize there is usually a drop associated with the dock. It might be under the dock or close to it.

236 "Expect fish to be shallow. When the sun hits the black plastic floatation, it warms the water some. The black crappie will suspend up at a foot to three feet under the surface in the warmer water. The fish might be at two feet in 40 feet of water.

237 "Hair jigs versus plastic? Hair jigs are good, and they catch crappie. But the plastic is so much cheaper, it's the popular choice. You can get a dozen plastic jigs for what one or two good hair jigs cost. Also, plastic is simpler to use and change."

238 Charles says, "Travis talked about jig weights, but it's important to note that when fishing together we are not using the same weight jigs. We are covering different water. Maybe he will be using a ¹⁄₁₆-ounce so I'll use a ¹⁄₃₂. His bait will be dropping down into deeper water and I'll be working the upper portion.

239 "Use high-vis line, and watch the bow. Look for the line jump by watching the middle of the bow in the line for any indication of a strike.

240 "In general, I crank two or three cranks of the handle then stop. Fish will react to just the change in speed.

241 “Look for wildcard spots. Dock owners often place brush around the outside of docks. Crappie like using these brushpiles in winter. Just get a bait to the strike zone no matter what depth that might be. You’ll catch fish.

242 “This part of the book is about shooting docks,” says Charles, “but don’t get hung up that docks are the only thing you can shoot. You can shoot a jig under trees, around pilings or any time you would be casting. Shooting gives better accuracy and keeps the bait low so it is less affected by the wind.

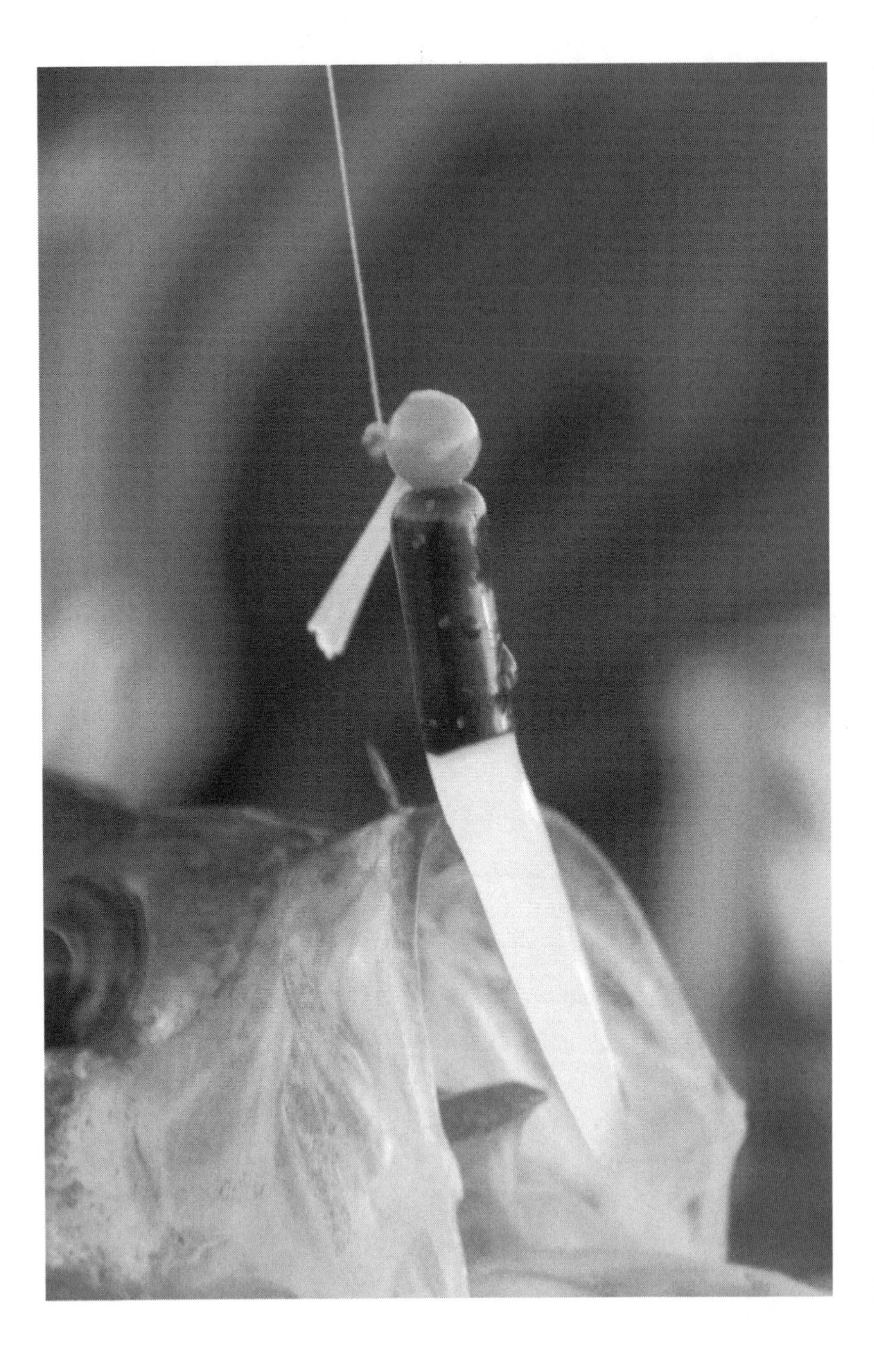

CHAPTER 12
ADVANCED ELECTRONICS

Electronic graphs can be simple (economical) or the latest high-tech (expensive). The good news is the prices have gone down. They are still a big investment, but for $600-$800, a loaded, high-tech 9-inch graph will provide everything needed for serious fishing. Learning all the features isn't easy, but they can be learned.

One tip for learning new electronics is to remove all the poles from the boat. Go to the lake with the graph's manual and spend time learning the unit and what it's showing. Knowing the menus, controls and adjustments improves a fisherman's efficiency and therefore improves catching. The reward is more fish per hour.

In 2018, the Buntings ran two Helix 12 Humminbirds with a 360 on the front one. Charles says, "We use Humminbird, but all companies have good units. Helix units sell for $600 while the new 15-inch units can cost $3500. Then add the cost of a 360 for another $1000. The best front and back electronics can easily run $8000. But remember, you can still get the much less expensive electronics that will do the job."

Having a section devoted to electronics may seem extreme. Some budgets only allow for a basic unit. Some of the following tips apply to all units while others refer only to advanced models.

"We've used Humminbird Side Imaging units for a long time," says Travis. "They've been instrumental in us finding more fish and more structure. For example, we fished an Oklahoma tournament and found a lot of brushpiles we would never have found with just a locator. We probably caught 200 fish the day of the tournament. It's not difficult to learn and use if you are good with a standard locator."

Charles says, "We got a big jump start because Travis got in early with Side Imaging and learned it well."

243 Travis says, "The minimum for a weekend fishermen is sonar and mapping/GPS. Today that's just a few hundred dollars. All of the sonar stuff made today is good, and the mapping will let a fisherman find spots to fish. He can also mark good fishing spots and beds to come back to later.

244 "Electronic maps are so much better than paper because they are updated many more times than the paper maps that become dated. Decent units for a reasonable price can be bought.

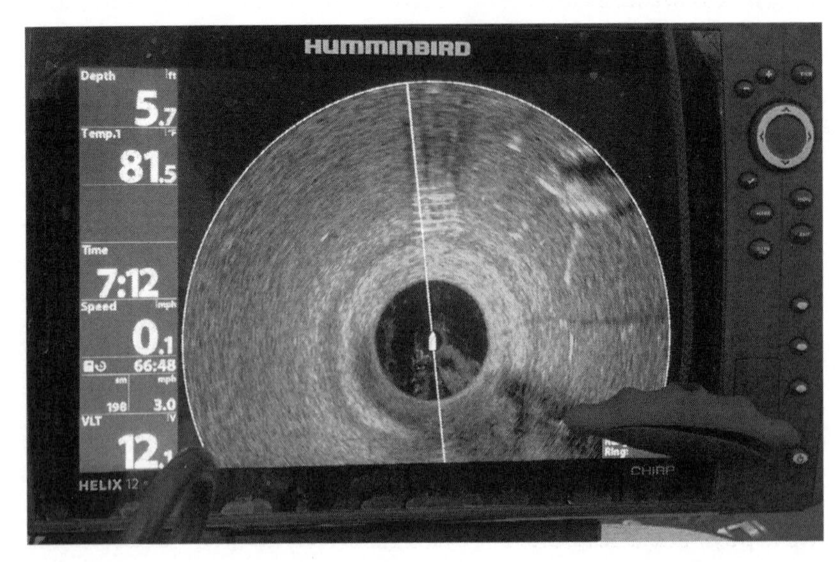

245 "On buying a locator, I would suggest getting the best you can based upon how serious you are. A man can fish with a Zebco 33 on a glass pole all his life, catch fish and be happy. When he upgrades to a $40 BnM pole, he won't go back to the glass pole. If he upgrades to a $200 pole, he won't go back to the $40 one. True with locators or anything else. We can upgrade, but it's difficult to downgrade.

246 "If you see a treetop, you can stop it on the graph, zoom in on the top, see the limbs on the brushpile and see the number of fish on it. Side Imaging covers a wide path to see more spots quickly."

247 Travis continues, "If you see something that doesn't have fish on it, you might as well go on because you won't catch anything. I've seen regular locators lie and show fish when really there is nothing but small limbs. A quality locator today won't do that.

248 "So a primary advantage of better electronic, like Side Imaging, is less wasted time. You don't need to fish water that doesn't have fish. Because you can see individual fish on a single log or in a thick brushpile, you know how many fish are there, and can decide if you want to fish it.

249 "Another huge advantage is finding bait schools with Side Imaging. If there are any around, they can be found by scanning 140 feet on a pass compared to 15 or 20 feet with traditional sonar.

250 "Pay attention to the bottom. Any locator will show the difference in hard and soft bottoms. A bottom can make as much difference as fishing in clear versus muddy water. That's one thing we always pay attention to when fishing.

"Watch for transition bottoms. A transition bottom can be a good spot for crappie. For example, the edge where a muddy bottom turns into a hard or rocky bottom.

251 "Look for multiple structures. Fence rows are good because most farmers piled rocks against the fence. Not only do you have a fence line with trees, you also have a hard bottom. You have wood, rocks and muddy bottom. It should be good.

252 "Any locator shows contour changes, and small changes can mean big results. A four- to six-inch contour change will not be noticed by most fishermen. They might catch fish at a set of trees and never know why. If you pay very close attention and see the small changes in the bottom, it can mean the difference between fish and no fish.

253 "Consider Humminbird 360 if you are very serious about your fishing. It scans even when the boat isn't moving. It shoots a full circle and gives a clear image. When spider rigging, you can see the fish and see your baits. You can see a school of bait and the fish so it's easy to follow that school of fish. In a lake like Truman, you see some stumps with the locator, but with 360, you see the stump, where the tree fell into the lake, the branches and where fish are located, so you know where to put your baits.

"While jigging today, we were in shallow water but were seeing a crystal-clear picture of what was beside our boat. We probably fished 150 stumps, caught two fish, and both were on stumps with smaller submerged structure on them. We wouldn't have caught a fish if not using the 360. We were seeing stuff that was under the water within pole length of the boat. We would see it and drop a jig on it. Side Imaging is great, but you can't run it in three feet of water in stumpy areas like we were fishing.

254 "Learning 360 or Side Imaging? There is a learning curve. People go out and buy a high-dollar Side Imaging or 360 unit or anything with advanced options but then they don't go out and learn how to use what they bought. I can buy the fanciest computer in the world, but it doesn't make me a computer pro. It is a tool that has to be learned.

255 "The first Side Imaging we had was a 997, and I logged many hours using it. I wasn't looking at it the whole time, but I was a lot. When we sold our boat, they looked at the outboard motor and saw 50 hours of the 120 hours was idling. That was due to all the scanning.

"Here is our normal tactic for using electronics," says Charlie. "We start by using Side Imaging. We set it at 50 or 60 feet out the sides because the detail is better the less the scan distance. That's important. We look for structure because the detail is better.

We use GPS waypoints to mark what we find. We go back, set up for fishing and go into the covers we've marked. We have 360 Imaging so we see what's ahead, but any fisherman can ease up to a GPS spot and use sonar or down imaging. We are trolling into the structure.

"In 2019 we use Helix and Solex. Bigger is better, but even with a seven-inch unit, a fisherman can still find the most important stuff and see if fish are on it. The Helix is easier to use because we left ours on default most of the time and it worked great. The new Solex requires sensitivity to be changed often, probably because it has more power. We turn the sensitivity down in shallower water and turn it up in deeper. The extra power gives an outstanding picture.

"Example, if we were going to Sardis for the first time, in April, we would start by going to the upper part in the timber and follow the creek channel. The channel ledges will have logs and other wood that is on or just off the channel. We will see it with Side Imaging. Because it's in Mississippi, we will be slow trolling, pushing baits into the cover," continues Charlie.

"We spend a lot of time graphing. When prefishing for a tournament, if I find a good pattern, like brush on the top of 12-foot ledges, I may spend a full day doing nothing but running my graph marking these type spots. A recreational fisherman doesn't need to do that, but if they would spend more time looking for just the right spots to fish, they would eliminate a lot of unproductive fishing.

"It's important to note that just buying good electronics and putting them on the boat won't make you a better fisherman. You have to learn how to use them and put them to full use to find the right spots. It's like buying a trolling motor and never putting it in the water. A graph is a tool. If used, a fisherman can spend more time catching fish instead of just fishing."

Travis says, "Electronics change all the time, and 2019 brought major improvements. Humminbird has come out with 360 HD. Moving up to High Definition is a big improvement to something that was already very good.

"The biggest news is Garmin's LiveScope. It's changing fishing, no doubt. Fishermen are using it primarily for single-pole jig fishing. A fisherman can literally put a jig on a fish's nose and make him eat it. We went to Lake Fork, couldn't catch fish on the spots Dad had found in practice, went to our search mode and put 15.5 pounds in the boat using one-pole each and artificial bait only. A lot of fish we caught we would not have put a jig close to them if it hadn't been for LiveScope. Why? Because we were fishing stumps we couldn't see and the water temperature was 65 degrees so typically we would have been pounding shallow water. We were catching fish at 18 feet deep in 20 feet of water. I would have never dropped a jig that deep in prespawn water.

"And we could literally pick the size fish we were going to catch. Some fish would take maybe four minutes to catch. I wouldn't have kept a jig there if we couldn't watch the fish.

"It's getting to the point that tournament fishermen are going to look for 10 good fish a day and only catch the tournament-size fish. That's scary."

Is this hard on the fishery? Travis says, "It's possible if enough people get the units and learn to use them, they could target the biggest fish and hurt the big fish population in a lake. Electronics are so good, the long-term effect worries me a little."

Ranger

CHAPTER 13
ANCHORING TACTICS WITH POWER POLES

"After a fisherman is use to the Power Poles with Drift Paddles, they find them almost as important as electronics," says Charles. "We would not have won the Crappie Masters Classic without them because of the current in the river."

Power Poles are a specific brand of high-tech anchors. You see the long poles sticking up on the back of boats? Those are anchors. They can be deployed into the bottom of the lake to stop a boat in a specific spot. Their advantages over a manual anchor include less work, more accuracy in positioning the boat, fast deployment and quick removal from an anchored position. There are disadvantages including costs, weight and height.

"We love them," says Travis. "Power Poles have changed the way we fish because it has allowed us to fish shallow water and, be more consistent. A prime example was at a tournament we fished at Lake Conway in Arkansas. We fished a lot of six-foot water. We would go with the wind and when we got to where we wanted to fish, we would just drop the poles to stop us. We didn't need to have our trolling motor running in the spot. That makes a difference in shallow water.

"We won the Crappie Masters Classic on the river. We were fishing brushpiles. We were positioning ourselves and then putting the Power Poles down and working on the brushpile. If we had not had the Power Poles, we would not have won the tournament. We were fishing eddies so we were going into it, dropping the poles and holding our baits right in the brush."

256 Travis says, "The harder the wind blows, the more important the Poles are. If the wind is blowing hard, manual anchoring might be possible but not precise. Plus it's a lot of work.

257 "Be quiet when anchoring with any type of anchor. The spookier the fish the more important it is to be quiet.

258 "Poles hold you dead still in the wind. That's critical when putting baits into the brush. No other anchoring method can do that.

259 "Do not backwash a spot. If I'm really shallow, I will not hit my trolling motor unless it's a necessity. Go with the wind, move and ease the anchor or Power Pole back down. That way there is no noise and you don't have to backwash with the trolling motor to stop.

260 "The biggest mistake a fisherman can make is putting Power Poles on the boat and not using them. Learn to use them."

POWER POLE DRIFT PADDLES

Power Poles only reach so deep, around eight or nine feet for a 10-foot pole. The team uses them in a variety of ways to control their fishing. Paddles that attach to the poles help control steering and speed."

Travis says, "We use the paddles in deeper water to control our speed. Fishing is more efficient because we don't have to leave our fishing seats in front to adjust the speed of the boat. The same if we are using chains. We can use the Poles to lift them up and down. We get more fishing time during a day of fishing."

261 Charles says, "The Poles give us the advantage of chains but without all the work. Not everyone has Power Poles so they can use chains and get similar results. The key is slowing or stopping the boat.

262 "You can also use the poles to raise and lower a drift sock. It saves time and effort," says Travis.

263 "If we are running parallel to a bank while fishing and the wind is blowing perpendicular toward the bank, we'll turn our Paddles at an angle so when we move along fishing, the boat will stay parallel to the bank instead of the back end blowing in toward the bank. They give us boat control.

"They change the way we fish. We basically can anchor solid and quietly in shallow water. In open water we can slow our boat speed from 1.0 mile per hour to 0.5 mile per hour with the Paddles."

CHAPTER 14
BEDS ... PORCUPINE & OTHERS

"Learning where to put beds takes experience, along with experimenting," says Charles. "Finding the right places can take a lot of time graphing. We might spend a day looking but only take several minutes to put out porcupine beds. Putting out pallets or small trees can be very hard work; PVC is easy. Scrap pallets and stakes can usually be found for no cost, but the PVC is expensive."

PORCUPINE/PVC BEDS

"We fish a lot of different type beds, from brush to stakebeds to Porcupine PVC," says Charles. "It's unreal how the Porcupines hold fish.

"We are firm believers in the plastic. The beds work. We've won an Ozarks tournament from them. We've put them in Truman one day and caught fish on them the next. They'll work immediately but get better over time when they get a buildup on them. The minnows feed on algae, and crappie feed on the minnows."

"PVC does not always hold the numbers of crappie, but they seem to hold the biggest fish.

"We fished a Tunica Lake tournament and found a lot of Porcupines. We pulled up to one and actually caught 14 fish out of 16 hits. They were gar, catfish, white bass and crappie, but we had 14 fish on.

"We got lucky and won Lake of the Ozarks three years in a row by fishing plastic. We would fish it in the mornings there and catch nothing but go back in the afternoon and tear them up. Sun, clouds, shadows and angles all make a difference. Where you set them is obviously very important, like a ledge, flat or whatever. If they are in shallow water, a breeze blowing in or bright sunlight might pull them in to it.

264 "To build a Porcupine, start with the ball," says Charles. "We use our own PVC pipe. We are lucky to have some good access to scrap pipe. We cut the bottom center legs shorter than the others so there will be nine legs touching bottom to give it a better base to hold it steady.

265 "We use a lot of yellow pipe because we have access to it. The green you get with the kit is good too. When we buy we get the gray electrical because it's the cheapest. The pipe has to be ½-inch OD. We cut the pipe into the lengths we want. We often use 36 inches as our primary length, but even if they are shorter for shallow water, we will leave our horizontals at 36 inches.

266 "On the water, pipes are glued into the holes. We add two bricks for weight. That's plenty because the pipes fill with water and that helps stabilize the bed.

267 "Place the beds in spots you think will be good. Our placement is determined by the technique we will be using. If single-pole jigging, we'll look for a little drop in four to 12 feet of water. We'll put three of them together, so when we get to them, we'll have more of them to fish in a concentrated area. We've had good success with groups of beds.

268 "For slow trolling, we will put them four to 16 feet deep. We will put them in a row or line from shallow to deep. If the bed is six feet tall in 14 feet of water, fish will likely be seven to 12 feet deep on it because they like to hang around near the top and edges.

269 "Look for a spot that is close to a successful spot. Place beds within 50 yards of that spot.

270 "Use PVC so the bed will last forever. They are also easier and safer to place. They create fewer hangups when fishing so it makes them great for family fishing.

271 "Jim Dant won two tournaments on Truman Lake from beds. He added weight to them but also used a rope to tie to them and then to trees. He puts them next to good cover. We don't do it because the beds are so easy to find, but they do work great and a lot of fishermen do that on Truman."

OTHER BEDS

PVC works great but can be expensive. The Buntings also use stakes to make wooden beds. The placement theories are the same.

Charles says, "Each lake is different. We place 90 percent of our beds in 12 feet of water or less with just a few down to 16 feet. This makes them easy to fish, and they work on our lake all year long.

272 "Find a small drop of one or two feet and place some beds on it.

273 "Not all beds will work. We've placed them on perfect drops with little other cover and they don't pull fish. Just know that some you put out won't work.

274 "Use your electronics. Every fisherman should put out beds, but you'll also find others to fish. Turn your sensitivity up and you'll find the beds, even the PVC.

275 "Build small beds. If you have a huge bed, it might take a while to really figure it out when you get to it. Fish might only be in one small spot. On a small bed, if they are there you'll know it immediately."

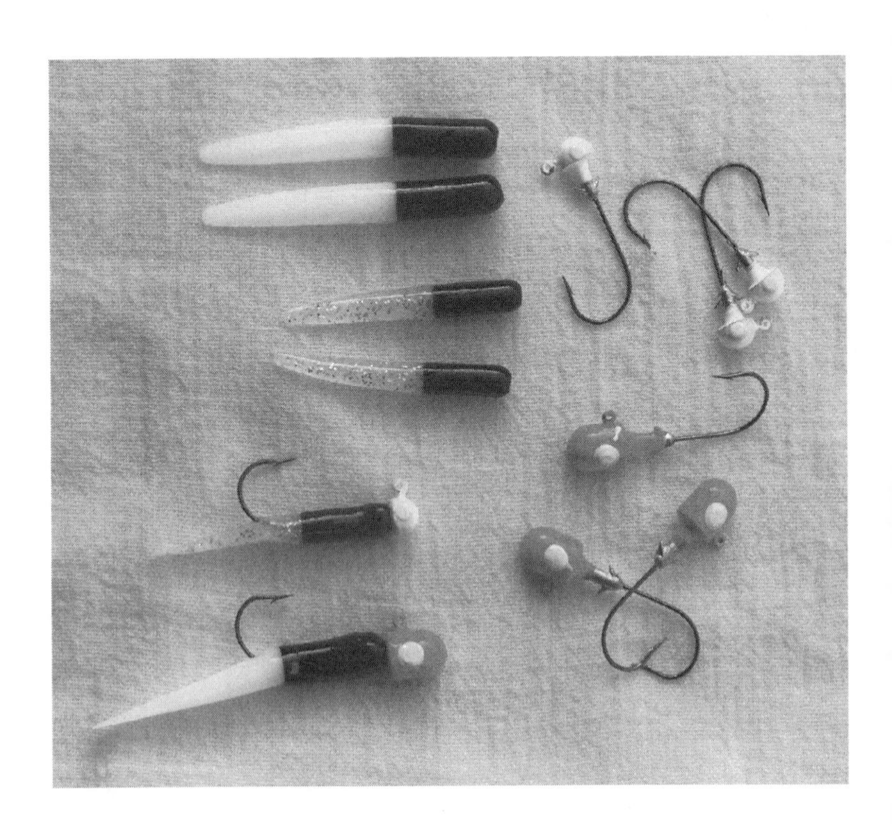

CHAPTER 15
MUDDY WATER BRAND BAITS

"It started when a bass buddy and me were using some of the thinner tail baits in the 2.5- and 3-inch size," says Travis. "Those soft baits had the problem of the tail catching on the hook point 40 percent of the time. Hooksets were a problem. Someone needed to make a bait for shooting docks so I ended up making my first mold out of wood. I basically used drill bits and did a little carving. It was just a tapered tail that looked like a cone. I heated up leftover baits and poured them in, then dipped them in another color and they worked pretty good. We knew the bait needed to be refined.

"A medium shiner is about 2.5 inches by ¼ by 5⁄16 across the back. That's what we went with on the jig measurements. If you stand a minnow up on edge the way a crappie normally sees it, and not a side profile, it's identical to the Muddy Water bait. A lot of people don't know that. You can fish it flat or upright. Being a solid-head bait, you can cut a little of the body off if you want a shorter jig.

"The primary purpose of the jig is skipping, and it does it well. We use a 1⁄16-ounce round head. The plastic solid body is good, and it can be bounced off the water and banged off the docks. It has to be tough," says Travis.

"There have been a few problems with the business from time to time but not many. One thing that's important is to not oversell inventory. The jigs have sold and we've had to work hard making them to stay up. With experience, we've learned how to balance everything. We want to be busy but not so busy not to have some family time.

"The best jigs are super-soft plastic. A harder plastic doesn't feel natural to the fish so they immediately spit it out. Soft is best, almost to the point of being mushy, but it won't last more than a bite or two. So we chose a plastic that was durable but soft enough to catch fish."

In 2019, there is a smaller 2-inch version available.

There are times when any jig will catch crappie. There are other times when the fish can be very picky. The Muddy Water Baits provide a unique design, brilliant colors and a built-in garlic scent that combines to make an offering many crappie like. The Buntings have plenty of trophies to back the jigs' effectiveness.

CHAPTER 16
MISCELLANEOUS TIPS, FISH KNOWLEDGE & HABITS

276 Charles says, "Visit the Grizzly Jig Show each year in Caruthersville, Missouri, the weekend before the Super Bowl. It's the best crappie-fishing show in the world. If you're looking for poles, they have every type pole you could ever want or need. They have all the plastic baits. It's the best crappie-fishing store in the country. During the big show, crappie fishermen from around the country are giving free seminars. You get to see and hear the best of the best. And these experts are on the floor to visit with you about baits, tackle and answer any fishing questions you have. It's great.

277 "Boat tip? I run a ¼-inch air line from the front to the back of the boat. I have my Mr. Bubblers in the back of the boat wired to my big battery. I have a switch to turn them off and on. So in the front of the boat where we are fishing, we have no noise while we aerate our minnows. Also, we don't have D-batteries going dead on us.

278 "Keep minnows cool. Any time the water temperature is over 70 degrees, you are killing your minnows. Keep the water cool, about 10 degrees cooler than the water that will be under 80 degrees when you're down a few feet.

279 "Keeping fish alive isn't always easy. Again, cool water is part of the system. We fish tournaments, so we must keep our fish alive. We keep the water cool and seldom run the circulator because the current stresses the fish. The fish will also lose weight because its belly will be pressured and it will expel stuff. Cool water and good aeration have worked great for us.

280 "Tips for a fun trip to a new lake? If a fisherman is going to recreational fish for three to five days, I suggest hiring a guide the first day. The guide will teach the technique and type areas where the fisherman can catch fish for the rest of the trip. It would be Todd Huckabee in Oklahoma, Barry Morrow in Missouri, Kyle Schoenherr in Illinois and John Harrison in Mississippi. They will teach you how to catch fish for the whole week you are there. With all the expenses of gas, motel and other things, it's a small investment for a fun week.

281 Charlie continues, "A weekend fisherman can take a 12- or 14-foot pole, walk the bank when fish are shallow and catch fish. This is especially true in spring.

282 "A beginning boat fisherman has a lot of trouble finding fish. That fisherman needs to study, listen and learn. Go to seminars. Talk to successful fishermen. Ask questions. Don't ask for spots but ask for patterns and maybe general areas of the lake. If you find out that fishermen are catching fish at 10 feet in a particular creek, you can go there and have a good chance of finding fish."

283 Be a teacher and help others. "I like to train and help others. Sonny Sipes was on the Alabama River telling us his Side Imaging wasn't worth a hoot. We have a nine-hour drive back home, but Travis gets in his boat after the tournament to help him set it up and teach him how to use it. On another lake, I jumped in a fisherman's boat one day, left mine floating in the lake and helped him with his Humminbird. He calls me later and tells me if he is finding stuff in his home lake he never knew was there. I like doing that for fishermen.

284 "Put away poles you are not using. It will eliminate a lot of accidents to the poles and give you more room in the boat. Wrap poles together when travelling to reduce vibrations and wear.

285 "Consider jigging poles with rear seats. They have better balance so they have a better feel. You'll detect more strikes, too.

286 "EVA foam handles may not have the feel of cork, but they work better in the rain and with fish slime. The foam also holds better in holders.

287 "A fisherman needs to learn one technique and use it until he is really good at it. If he tries to do a bunch of different techniques, but doesn't do them well, the catch is going to be disappointing. Pick one technique and use it all year until you are good. Then, in six months or a year, pick another technique and start learning it. You then have one technique you are good at while learning a second. Keep adding techniques as you learn to do each one well."

288 What do you do when not catching fish? "It's important to learn why. Part of that goes back to electronics. Learn to find different structure, always structure, and learn what the fish are relating to. We've learned that 90 percent of the time fish will be in structure.

289 "Knots are always a question at seminars. Many fishermen like a loop knot with a jig to give more action. I prefer a Palomar knot. I pull it back as far as I can to get it back toward the hook point. When you drop the bait straight down this keeps the hook up high so you are actually leading the bait down."

290 Travis says, "Fish around the roots of a stump. Depending upon how deep and how the stump is positioned, current will take the easiest path and might wash the dirt away from around the roots. You can see these on a locator, especially with Side Imaging. You can go in with a large ¼-ounce jig and feel the roots. These roots will likely be holding the biggest fish.

291 "Look for current breaks. A river tip starts with fishing eddies. When the current allows, the river itself has a lot of good ledges and timber. But, when there is current, you need to find bars and other places where eddies are formed that create slack water.

292 "At spawn time, there is nothing more important than water temperature. Spawning begins at 58 degrees. Something in the area, like a rock under the surface, might be the first place they hit because the rock draws solar heat."

293 How to take care of poles? "Very funny question because we are the world's worst at taking care of them. When we are fishing, we are going full speed. If we change from one set to another, we are in a hurry and slap them down instead of being careful. It's cost us because a pole will only take so much. However, it's not as bad as it sounds. We do put them in racks when traveling, tie them together and sometimes break them down and put them in the box to give us more room."

294 Travis discusses jig versus minnow. "A straight jig is great for reaction bites. Minnows are good for drawing bites from hungry fish. The smaller the minnow the more the vibration. The larger the minnow the bigger the profile and more scent. We tip our jig with a minnow out of habit, but sometimes it's not needed. We fish minnows all year long, but most of our fish come off jigs or jigs tipped with minnows.

"For me, if I have to wait five minutes holding a jig still, I'm not going to catch a fish. A minnow is easier to do that with, forcing me to slow down, especially with a straight minnow.

295 "If I'm jig fishing, I'll have two poles with different baits on them. I don't know how smart crappie are, but they do have memory. Sometimes they'll hit one bait and not the other. It's possible if they hit a jig and don't take it, I've got to drop a different look for him to be willing to bite again because he already knows he didn't have any luck with the first jig, but he is still hungry and might bite.

296 "Solid plastics versus hollow plastics. Solid plastic is more durable. After a bait slides down on the jig the fish won't bite it. Also, solid plastic can be slid up on a minnow hook.

297 "Critter plastics? They're too much. A fish is very simple. They live, eat and reproduce. You get all the fancy stuff that looks good in the package but it seldom catches more fish than simpler plastic."

298 Travis continues, "So many things can determine which color a crappie wants. Low light, even when fishing clear water, calls for a dark bait. It needs to be something that blocks out and creates a profile. In bright light when their vision is increased, I'll use something more natural looking. They don't need the sunlight blocked out to see the bait in bright conditions. In dark water, you need something to block the light so when they look up they see the bait profile.

299 "My top three colors are black-chartreuse glow, Outlaw (lime green and chartreuse glow) and white-chartreuse.

"I believe color is more about confidence than anything else. Somebody could fish beside me with a black-pink and catch as many as me, but I need to be confident in the color I'm fishing and that comes from success and experience. A confidence color.

300 "I don't match jigheads to body colors. We use an orange head 99-percent of the time in clear or stained water. Orange holds its color deeper than any other color. The biggest deal is that we use to carry every color head and ended up catching as many or more on orange, so instead of carrying all those heads in every color, we simplified down to orange."

301 The minimum jig pack needed? "Black-chartreuse jig body works just about anywhere we go. When a fisherman does not get a bite for a while it is possible the fish have keyed in upon one specific color. However, you don't want to change all the time When it gets slow for a while, you'll start losing confidence in whatever color you have on."

FISH KNOWLEDGE & HABITS (WITH TRAVIS)

302 Crappie: Homies & Travelers. "Fish are a lot like birds," says Travis. "You've got your home birds and your travelers. I think there are fish that probably don't leave a 100-yard circle their whole life. Other fish will move 10 miles in a week. The bed can be slick at 9:00 in the morning and go back at 2:00 and it looks like a snowcone because the fish are jammed so tightly on it. You can light them up when it's like that. If you just go by the beds and fish the ones that are active, you'll catch a lot more fish by not fishing ones that are not going to produce."

303 Feeding cycles. "I learned a lot from watching fish in a 130-gallon fish tank I had. I caught three crappie 13 to 14 inches long and put them in the tank. I put the fish in and counted out 96 minnows into the tank. For three days those fish did not touch a minnow. On the third night, I looked the next morning and there was not one minnow left in the tank. I believed it was the shock of being pulled from a stained pond and put into a clear-water tank. They got hungry and gorged themselves on day three.

"I put more minnows in and the crappie stayed on a two- or three-day pattern of not eating and then gorging. I noticed that on the lake during a drought that the fish did the same thing. A drought is consistent being hot, humid and no fronts. Tuesday might be great but awful on Saturday and good on Sunday. There were no fronts to blame. So fish in the tank and lake did about the same thing. There was no reason why some days were good and some were not, but the fish were on a cycle."

304 Crappie feed up … and down. "Another thing I experimented with," says Travis, "were jigs. I cut the hooks off. The first thing I tested was the fact crappie always feed up. That's wrong. I would put the jig on bottom. The crappie would stand straight up, go down and suck the jig up and then return to their normal position.

"Another interesting thing they did was when they took a bait off bottom. My aquarium had a rock bottom with very small rocks. They would suck the bait in then blow water out to flush the gravel that they picked up from the bottom of the tank. That would back flush their gills to clean them.

305 "The bait is important. When the hardness of the plastic was a little hard or the size of the head too big, the jig was coming right back out their mouths. I could put the same bait back into the tank a month later and the fish would come up to it but would not eat it. I could change color and profile and the fish would hit it every time.

306 "We preach patterns, but on many river systems, patterns are out the door. Moving water is different. When we won at Columbus, we hit one spot in 2.5 feet of water, the next might be in 16 feet, and then in eight feet. We had a pattern in the sense we

were fishing structure out of the current, but every day there were places that were eliminated because the water was falling rapidly, changing the current patterns that would eliminate some of our spots. The changing water added new spots, but we had to go find them. Our pattern was structure outside the current, but it wasn't structure in eight feet of water.

307 "Lakes versus rivers? If I'm on a lake and get into gar or catfish I don't catch crappie. If I'm on a river, I don't worry about it because they all swim together. It can actually be a good thing, but be sure to have three or four times the minnows you normally use because the gar will eat them up."

308 "Something tournament and recreational fishermen have in common is knowing the importance of a laydown, or fallen tree. How good a tree is for fishing is determined by many factors. How many limbs does it have? How are the limbs positioned? What depth of water is it in? Is the top in at least 20 feet of water? If not, is it deep enough for the season?"

309 Charles says, "Start fishing a laydown on the deepest, outside edges. I like casting to a laydown, but we will slow troll it, too. When casting, use a weedguard so you won't stay hung all the time and the jig can walk over the limbs. What you are doing is pulling over the limbs, and, when the jig comes over and falls, it triggers a bite.

310 "If a fisherman prefers a minnow. Then the slip-float is best. It's more difficult than fishing a jig but it works. The point is, a laydown is outstanding and can be fished different ways."

PRO STAFF

CHAPTER 17
TOURNAMENTS, PREFISHING & RECREATIONAL FISHING

311 Apply tournament tactics to your recreational fishing. Charles says, "At a new lake, I'll start at the upper end and work my way down. The bigger fish are usually located in the upper part of the lake. We are here at a tournament and I have no idea where I will end up fishing. I have started in shallow water and worked my way out to 14 feet to see where the most active and larger fish are located. In 14 feet, the fish are suspended over the stumps. We have a cold front that will be dropping air temperatures from the 80s to the 50s. I believe the fish in deeper water will be more likely to bite after the front. I'll use my graph to find and mark the exact places I want to fish."

312 How long do you stay with a game plan that isn't working? "One or two hours at the most if it's not working. We'll switch to something else. An example was at the Washington tournament and we were fishing Lee. We trolled at 0.2 and 0.3 mile per hour, but at 10:00 we had two small fish. Travis asked me to get the 16-foot Pro Staff poles and put 2-ounce weights on them. We put those poles out, picked up our speed to 1.2- and 1.5-mile-per-hour and started catching the shallow fish that wouldn't bite the slow presentation. So yes, we change game plans quickly if we are not catching fish."

313 Travis says, "Light penetration is a big thing because crappie have sensitive eyes. Lake of the Ozarks is a good example. A big storm went through that night, and it was overcast the next morning. We went through our beds and caught a few small fish, maybe one tournament fish. Later the sun came out and I told Dad we needed to fish them again. He didn't want to because we didn't do good the first time. But the light penetration meant the fish could see the baits better, and we caught six of our seven weigh-in fish on the second run through the beds. Instead of catching six or seven fish, we caught 40 or 45 better fish. Light penetration was the difference."

314 Charles says patterns are important. "The biggest mistake of a weekend fisherman is not learning a pattern. They spot fish old spots. If the fish aren't in their four or five spots, they think the fish aren't biting. It could be they have moved to another depth. Check different areas, depths and structures to form a pattern.

315 "If we are prefishing on waters we know, we don't fish spots we know we will fish during the tournament because we don't want to pull fish off them. We are looking for places to add on to our list for the tournament. If we need a place to go the last hour and a half and know we have a good chance to pull a couple of big fish, it's a huge advantage.

"Kyle Schoenherr is a prime example. Here at Truman, he is here for four or five days prefishing. He will likely spend three of those days studying his graph. He knows the general areas and type stuff he wants to fish. So, he turns on his electronics and scouts to find the fish and spots to fish. He might hit one out of 10 or 15 spots just to see the size of the fish, but that's it. He won't fish on Friday what he plans to fish on Saturday during the tournament. A lot of people make the mistake of staying in areas they plan to fish tournament day."

316 Charles continues, "We prefish a lot with our electronics. We go by our beds to see if fish are on them and will come back to them on tournament day. If people see us catch a fish, they'll find and fish it. We believe it will take those fish three days before they bite again.

"Winning tournaments can lead to problems. We have people watching and coming by to find our spots. At Lake of the Ozarks, they put spotter boats on us to GPS and learn where we were catching fish because nobody knew for a few years where we were fishing."

317 Maximize your time on the water even when recreational fishing. "Fishermen often spend too little time at a spot when checking for fish. We can't catch as many fish as the locals and fishermen who have fished a lake several times if it comes down to spot fishing. We have to figure out patterns. At Conway we had three hours left to practice so we went to the other lake that was included in the tournament. I rolled a good fish out of a brushpile in 12 feet of water. I caught another one out of a 12-foot brushpile. With limited time, I put my rods down and spent the next couple of hours using my electronics to find every brushpile I could find at 12 feet. On tournament day we went from GPS spot to spot. That's maximizing time.

318 "At a tournament in Columbus, Mississippi, everything was changing so much daily we got up at 3:00 A.M. in the morning and I slept in the boat while Travis found structure we could fish that day. We spent a lot of hours on the water.

319 Travis says, "Fishing beds? A recreational fisherman can find a good bed and have a good time. It might replenish some and be good for days. But when others see someone catching fish, they'll remember the spot and return to fish it.

320 "A fisherman might struggle working and doing his own thing when a group of boats are in an area catching fish. However, if he sticks with it long enough, he will gain much knowledge and become a better fisherman who can adapt to catch fish in almost any situation, not counting on others to lead him to fish."

DO YOU ALWAYS CATCH FISH?

Charles says, "We are here at Grenada Lake in spring. The lake has risen about 15 feet to 22 feet, which is about five feet above summer pool but way above winter pool where it should be right now. Fishing is tough. The water temperature has fallen for a week with 34-degree nights. The water is down to 54 degrees in most places. We have falling water temperatures, high water and strong wind, so it's tough fishing.

"I think part of the problem is the lake is so spread out now with all the water. The crappie are scattered out and back up in the brush where you can't get them. Our strategy has been to troll in about eight feet of water over grass beds that come up to five feet. We are still looking."

321 What to do when not catching fish? "I've changed speeds, baits, bait colors, downsized and fished different areas. I've been on fish but just haven't gotten them to bite. But doing those things ensures I'm not missing something that might trigger a bite. Usually it will, but not on this trip.

"Do we always catch fish? The answer is 'No'. Weekend fishermen need to know that. They may read about us, see us on TV or maybe on the water on a good day and think we come to a lake and just catch crappie. That's not the way it happens most of the time. This week I've averaged catching two fish a day here at Grenada and that's fishing all day working hard at it. I talked to three of the best guides on the lake and they are cancelling trips. Sometimes we don't catch fish."

322 What do you do the night before a big tournament? Charlie says, "Whether fishing for fun or a tournament, I'll be working to get the boat ready and tying rigs. Everything needs to be ready to fish before getting to the ramp.

"For a tournament, I try to get to bed at night between 8:30 and 9:00. Adrenaline is flowing. I'm usually tired by the time the tournament is here due to several hard days practicing so I do go to bed early every night. I get up before 5:00 A.M. Keeping a routine helps with sleeping.

"At a big tournament, there is registration, banquet, media fishing and they all take away from practice time, but that's part of it. We are sponsored so we have responsibilities, but that's okay because it's just part of the pro side of fishing."

323 Do you listen to "fish talk" from other fishermen? Charlie says, "Not at all. I take it with a grain of salt. I find my own fish.

You always hear a few fishermen say they are on fish catching a lot during practice, but they don't bring them to the weigh-in line."

324 What else is important? "A fisherman on the water needs to drink a lot of water. I get water, but I don't always eat. Both are important."

325 Game plan? "Of course, whether fishing for fun or a tournament. You need to have a plan. Sometimes when a plan doesn't work, we just stay with it if we believe in it. Sometimes we have to change."

STUFF HAPPENS

Reelfoot Lake. Things happen when traveling and on the road. Charles says they've been lucky overall. Maybe he has, but I remember mid-morning during a Reelfoot Lake tournament when they pulled into the restaurant with the boat and trailer in tow. These are serious fishermen, so I was surprised.

A trip to their boat removed all doubt. There was a gash from near the front all the way to the back. "We tore the bottom out of the boat," says Charlie. "We think it was a railroad spike driven into the top of a stump that fishermen tie trotlines to. It didn't give when we hit it."

The tear was 11 feet long, and they barely made it back to the ramp. The boat was not repairable.

Truman Lake. The team was in the top after day one. "We blew our lower unit out on day two," says Charles. "I called my wife and had her bring us another boat. There were no electronics on it. We lost two or three hours of fishing and dropped down but stayed in the top ten. We couldn't fish our beds because we had no electronics. We should have taken time to add a graph but didn't."

Grenada Lake. Charles was meeting me at the ramp. He was late, and that's very unusual for him. I learned he had a flat on the trailer, changed it, skipped breakfast and was at the ramp just slightly behind schedule. On the road, stuff happens, but hopefully it's something simple like a tire.

On the Road. "When on the road, we try to carry everything we need for emergencies and be prepared," says Charlie. "Sometimes things just happen. When traveling for tournaments, the other guys are competitors on the water but your best friends when you need help. We all depend upon each other when we need help."

WATER

CHAPTER 18
TRAVIS ... ON WINNING

CRAPPIE MASTERS CLASSIC

Travis says, "It was the first time we had been to Tombigbee. We just showed up a week ahead of time, turned on the locater and started fishing. In prefishing, at that time, we ran a 1198 Humminbird on the console, and we probably spent 25 percent of our time fishing and 75 percent of our time using our electronics to mark spots.

"Day-one tournament game plan was to fish the river and stay on the move. The water conditions were changing, and the river didn't have consistent patterns. It wasn't like a lake. We spot fished in the river with one spot being three feet, the next one at 18 feet and the next one at six feet. We started at the furthest spot from the ramp and planned to run-and-gun all the way back to the ramp. It was about 20 miles. After weigh-in on day one, we were in fifth place, but the weights and fish weren't big there so we didn't think anyone would make a huge jump the next day like you can see at Grenada. We just decided to try to improve a little on day one's weight and hopefully make a run.

"We were fishing structure so we were going through 50 or 60 new rigs a day. On day one we wanted to hit up to 35 spots and push the limitations on how many spots we could fish. I didn't want to hit them hard but make it more like a prefishing day, but we were keeping our big fish. The plan was working great but we had a big fish stressed out and had to quit early on day one.

"On day two we only fished the spots where we had caught a big fish the day before and fished them slowly and methodically. We wanted to fish every twig. Day two a cold front came in so it worked well with our plan to fish slowly. I didn't think they could have gotten buried deeper in the brush, but they did on day two.

"The 6.5 inches of rain scared most fishermen off the river. But fishing is like hitting a baseball: when you feel it, you just feel it and you put streaks together. We felt it was where we needed to be. When things are going wrong in fishing, it's just like being on a cold streak in baseball when you can't do anything right.

"On tournament day, whoever makes the most correct decisions usually will be the winner. Go or stay, where next? Stay within your limits. What helped us in the classic was to cut down to six rods instead of eight. The number of places we fished with putting poles out and putting them up again over and over, so it gave us more time fishing and it worked.

"The mental aspect is like anything else in life. When you have confidence you'll do a better job. I don't mean arrogance. If you believe stuff you are fishing will produce seven fish a day, you need to stick with it. What I've done in past years when plan A didn't work and the hair started standing up a little on my neck, and when plan B and C didn't work, the rest of the day was spent running around like a chicken with its head cut off. It's easy to panic and fish too fast. Part of the mental game is to stay calm and fish slowly even though you may be running full speed from the time you start pulling up your poles to head to the next spot and get them back into the water again. When I get into a bind, I try to remember back when I've had a similar situation and it turned out good.

"A few years back when fishing a tournament at Dardanelle, we had awesome prefishing, catching big fish after big fish. On tournament day at 1:30, we had one tournament fish in the boat. I told Dad we have one spot where we only caught little fish the day before, but it's all we had left. We pulled over the spot, and seven or eight poles went down. They all had 1.5-pound plus fish on them. It was crappie nirvana. I can look back on that day and remember it happened right at the end of the day. It gives a mental edge knowing it is possible it can happen again. You're tired, weather might be bad, and things don't look good so it's easy to give up.

"In this classic we won, nothing made us happier when the heavy rains came and the river kept running water and stayed high. It didn't matter people had been practice fishing for a month because everything changed."

Many of the ideas and tips on winning certainly apply to recreational fishing. Make good decisions and stay within your limits. Do what you do and do it right. Also, remember that fish can turn on at any time so don't get discouraged. Following fish movements and patterns is great, but sometimes conditions turn sour and you need to fish it like it's a new lake or river.

WINNING THE AMERICAN CRAPPIE TRAIL (ACT) NATIONAL CHAMPIONSHIP

ACT Classic, National Championship 2017, Lake of the Ozarks, Missouri.

Travis says, "Dad got to prefish all week, but I was working. He stayed away from our main spots. On the last day of practice when we both fished, because he didn't catch good fish anyplace else, we went into the areas we like to fish. We were just trying to establish a pattern. We fished deeper than we had ever fished there, going to 13 to 16 feet. We don't like deep water, but we got on a pattern and caught two big fish in two spots.

"We started running other patterns in different places, trying to establish a backup plan. Because there were so many fishermen from many different states who had never fished the place before, you get a lot more people graphing and looking for places to fish. Although local fishermen usually stick to their own stuff, we had out-of-town fishermen who found many of our spots so it cut down some of our fishable water."

The team decided to run-and-gun spider rig like they often do, going faster than normal and covering as much water as possible. Their game plan worked, and they were leading after day one.

Travis said there were some stories about people catching nine to nine-and-a-half pounds, but Travis told his dad not to worry because those fishermen were done. The spots weren't replenishing, or restocking, quickly so those places wouldn't win the tournament. That proved true for the Buntings during the tournament because they couldn't catch tournament-size fish on day two where they caught them on day one..

"We stayed on the move," says Travis. "Where we caught 25 to 30 fish with two good keepers on day one, on day two we caught eight to 10 fish with no keepers. So we stayed on the move and covered a lot of water.

"About a month before the tournament, we found a bunch of natural cover. I spent eight or 10 hours with the graph marking it. That made a difference during the tournament because we had to switch to it. Our stuff wasn't producing, or it had other fishermen fishing it."

Would the team have changed anything? "Hind site is wonderful. We would have avoided plastic. It usually catches the biggest fish, but that never happened during the tournament. I don't know why the bite wasn't as good on the plastic."

The Buntings have won Classics with Crappie USA, Crappie Masters and American Crappie Trail. "Each one was very different and very important in different ways. It means a lot any time you win a classic."

MORE ON THE ACT CHAMPIONSHIP

ACT was on the Buntings' home lake. How important was that?

Charles says, "Home lakes can help and hurt. Sometimes, because of history, you think you know the best places to fish and miss checking all the lake. You outguess yourself.

"We have about 200 porcupine attractors and stake beds. On the second day of the tournament, realizing several are placed near each other, about half were covered with fishermen. Most were fishermen who had never fished these areas but found them with their electronics because they are good fishermen. They didn't see us on them. We went back to brush fishing like we do.

"We used 12-foot BnM Ultralights, spider rigging instead of using 16-foot poles because we wanted to stick the poles up tight into the brush and logs. For example, Travis went by a submerged tree and said there was fish on the rootwad. We caught a fish out of it on the first day.

"Day two started when we met the TV crew at 5:00AM and worked with them. We got a spotter in the boat and had an hour before start time. We used our electronics to look for laydowns in 12 to 14 feet of water. We caught four of our seven weigh fish on our home lake on cover we had never fished before. Side Imaging helped us find them, and a Humminbird 360 helped us catch them.

"Our stuff we found was upriver on channel breaks. Most were logs that had floated in. Having a rootwad seem to be very important for holding fish. We had 20-mile-per-hour wind so it created problems for many teams, but we were using our Power Poles and Drift Paddles and had no problem," says Charlie.

"It's funny now because fishermen being on the cover we intended to fish forced us to find other cover that had bigger fish on it. Any time you win a classic, you've got to know what you are doing but have to have some luck. Those fishermen who were fishing the cover we wanted to fish were our lucky break.

"Winning a classic is a sensation I can't explain. We are the only team to win a classic in each major circuit and I've very proud of that."

HOW TO WIN A CLASSIC

What does it take to win a classic?

Travis says, "If you look at the classic winners, you might see one or two teams who happened to have just the right lake for the technique they fish. But most of the time, it will be won by the fishermen who get out before daylight and stay until dark. Basically, it's the team who works harder than the other teams.

"When there are 150 teams in a classic it often comes down to one or two bites that make a difference. You have to put yourself in the right run size of fish that might win the tournament with those one or two bites.

"You have to have the skill to find and catch those fish, but having one or two kicker fish that wins a tournament requires luck be on your side. The tournament we won was on a 25-mile stretch of river. You have to put yourself in the right position to win, make good decisions and have many things go right for you."

250
Pro
POWER-POLE
SHALLOW WATER ANCHOR
SWIFT. SILENT. SECURE.
Ranger
BOATS
POWER-POLE
SHALLOW WATER ANCHOR
SWIFT. SILENT. SECURE.
Ranger
BOATS

CHAPTER 19
PROFILES

TEAM BUNTING, CHARLES & TRAVIS

Home town: Jefferson City, Missouri

Home lake: Ozarks, Truman in Missouri

Sponsors: Ranger, Mercury Motors, BnM Poles, Humminbird, Minn Kota, BnM Poles, Muddy Water Baits, Whack'em Jigs, Off-Shore Tackle, Tite-Lok, BalzOut, Missouri Goldfish, Engle Coolers, Dub-L-Seat, Porcupine, Southern Pro Tackle, Vicious Line and Ellis Batteries.

Tournaments through 2018: 2005 Crappie USA Classic Champs; 2006 Crappie USA regional win; 2007 National Points Title; 2009 Crappie Masters Mississippi State Championship; 2011-2013 three Crappie Masters Lake of the Ozarks wins in a row; 2012 Crappie Masters National Classic Championship; 2013 Crappie Masters Sportsmen of the Year; 2017 Eufaula Oklahoma Crappie Masters; 2017 American Crappie Trail National Championship; 2018 Lake Washington Crappie Masters.

Highlight/Memory: Charles says, "Without a doubt it has been getting to spend time with my son. I'm glad we've won some big tournaments. We've got to travel, compete together and make many new friends. As far as awards, the Sportsman of the Year award was very special."

Travis says, "Winning the first classic. I was never nervous while fishing, but when it was over, I realized what happened and the nerves started firing off. Dad was gone a long time for the polygraph, and even though we didn't do anything wrong, I started worrying about that. Everything was good, of course, but my mind got racing, people were congratulating, and it was an overwhelming happy, nervous experience."

Strength: "Every lake in the country is different so we must be versatile," says Travis. "We fish how we want to fish. If we go chasing ghosts or trying to fish the way everyone else is fishing instead of what we know best, we would be in trouble. The hardest fish to catch is someone else's fish. We hear a lot of stories at tournaments but we stick to our game plan. We do what we can do best on tournament day.

"Being versatile," says Charles. "We try to do whatever it takes to catch fish. I'm solid in fishing, but Travis has an out-of-the-box thinking that really helps us adjust to situations."

Favorite lake: Travis says "Any lake with structure. Truman when it's hot weather. Ozarks when it's cold. If I could fish any lake, it would be Dardanelle Arkansas. The upper end is a river system and lower end a lake. It's challenging because of fluctuating water and I like that challenge."

Charles says, "Grenada because of the big fish. And Truman Lake, especially for single-pole fishing."

Team goals. (Discussed before winning the ACT 2017 classic.) You've won two classics, regional and state championships. What are your goals now? Charles says, "I want to win more tournaments because I'm competitive. The chance of winning another classic is slim just because of all the good fishermen on the trail. Our job is to promote sponsors, and I enjoy that side of it. I enjoy talking to people and teaching. That's rewarding. I spend 20 to 25 days doing seminars and promoting. That's a goal when I retire, I want to do more of. I want to teach people in the boat how to use electronics, Power Poles and other things that will help them catch more fish.

"We fish tournaments for the enjoyment," Charles continues. "I've been the luckiest person in the world to travel with my son, now 37 years old. I've fished hundreds of hours in the boat with him. We might not get along all the time in the boat because we have different ideas what we need to be doing, but at the end of the day, we have a bonding that is important."

When Travis was asked his goals? "Win, Baby, Win!"

CHARLES BUNTING PROFILE

Charles was born in 1953. He retired from Embarq Telephone Company. He is known for being helpful to others and being a great representative of the sport.

He started by fishing an Embarq company tournament with a friend of his. That was in the 1980s. Charles joined a newly formed Capital City Crappie Club and says the older fishermen there taught him how to fish. He has fished national tournaments since about 1998.

"I love competition. I played competitive softball and basketball until my early forties.

Charlie says it's not just the competition. The crappie-fishing trail is like a family. He sees tournament friends a few times a year or maybe once every two or three years, but the friendships are very important to him.

When not working, he spends as much time as possible with his grandkids.

Fishing hero? "Not really but Ronnie Capps and Steve Coleman are definitely icons."

Pet peeves in fishing? "There are people who lie and I don't like that. They think they are bass fishermen or something. I don't like jet skis, but I stay away from lakes when they are there."

Boat food? "Deer sticks and jerky."

Sports teams? "Cardinal baseball. Chiefs but I'm not a big football fan.

What about your wife, Connie? "We've been married 45 years, and she has supported me in everything I do. When we got married, I was playing competitive baseball and basketball. She would always cook for several of our team members. She has been with Travis and me in all of our tournament fishing and the things we do. Like today, she is here at Grizzly Jig selling baits. She is the backbone of our team."

How would you like to be known/remembered? "As somebody friendly who would help anyone who asked. A fisherman who gave seminars and helped teach people how to fish."

TRAVIS BUNTING PROFILE

Travis was born 1979. His work includes union carpenter and owner of Muddy Water Baits. He has recently married.

He was little when he started fishing with his dad. They would go to Truman, tie to a tree and hope to get a bite. He got older and started bass fishing because it was a much cooler thing to do. After high school, his Dad started fishing crappie tournaments and doing well so he tried crappie fishing again.

After returning to crappie fishing, he learned he enjoyed it a lot more than bass fishing, and he enjoyed having something to eat at the end of the day. He and a buddy finished seventh in their first crappie tournament. They won enough money to afford to go to the regional in Oklahoma and finished sixth. They had money from that to go to the classic at Pickwick-Wilson. They arrived with four six-foot poles, had never fished a river system and had never heard of spider rigging.

He and his dad decided to fish together starting in 2003. They won their first classic, Crappie USA, in 2005 at Patoka, Indiana. They had learned spider rigging and combined some of the techniques they already knew. It worked.

Travis says barometric pressure, wind from the east and other factors are things to deal with, but he can't wait for a perfect day because he has to go fishing on days he has off. He works hard to find fish each day no matter the conditions. The conditions are not excuses for not catching fish.

He likes to keep rolling through different depths, patterns, areas of the lake and different baits until he finds a pattern. He believes that every day there will be at least some fish bite.

He spends much of his spare time making baits and spending time with his kids. "I'm very competitive and enjoy fishing tournaments but priorities change when you have kids."

Fishing hero? "Not really; maybe bass fishermen Bill Dance, Jimmy Houston and Roland Martin years ago. It didn't take long to know that Capps and Coleman were the big dogs in crappie."

Pet peeve? "I've always believed that the first fisherman to the spot gets it. This lake (Truman) is getting to be the worst because if there are 50 trees in a line that I'm fishing and someone pulls into the end that I'm fishing towards, I don't agree with it. Also, we've been followed around and I don't agree with that either."

Boat food? "I usually don't eat. If I do it's a deer sausage stick or jerky."

Favorite teams? "I like Cardinals baseball and Chiefs football. I like college best, anything Missouri."

How would you like to be known/remembered? "Just as someone who was respectful. I remember back when I started tournaments there were some fishermen who seemed to think they were better than others. Dad and I have tried hard to never do that. We talk to anyone. We've tried to help others. I want to help people catch more fish."

APPENDIX
BUNTING EQUIPMENT LIST

Boat: Ranger Boat

Motor: Mercury

Trolling Motor: Minn Kota Ultrex

Anchors/Boat Control: 10′ Power Poles with Drift Paddles

Electronics: Humminbird Solix 15 on console. Humminbird Helix 12 on front deck. Humminbird 360 on trolling motor

Reels: BnM Pro 100 spinning reels

Poles: All BnM Pole Company
Slow Troll: 12′ BnM Ultralights; 16′ BnM BGJP jigging poles
Pulling Crankbaits with Planer Boards: BnM Silver Catfish
Jigging: 11′ Tree Trimmer; 12′ BnM Ultralight
Pitching: 6′ SharpShooter, 7′ Sam Heaton
Corking: 9′ BnM Float and Fly
Shooting: 6-6.5′ Richard Williams; 6′ Dock Shooter
Casting: 6′ Dock Shooter

"Concerning our jigging poles," says Charlie, "The BnM 12-foot Ultralight has always been one of our bread-and-butter poles. It's really lightweight and can be used for slow trolling, too. We can really see light bites and get a good hookset. A 2-pound fish can be hoisted into the boat, no problem. The newer model with a rear seat is great for jigging because of balance.

"We'll also be using the new 11-foot Tree Trimmer jigging pole. It's stiffer and can be an advantage in feeling more bites and getting fish into the boat. It's stronger but still lightweight so it can be used for jigging without wearing you out."

Pole Holders: Driftmaster. The newest singles with full adjustment on top and bottom. A setup in the back allows for pulling crankbaits or jigs.

LINE

Slow Trolling: Vicious high-visibility 12-lb main line; 8-lb-test leaders

With Planer Boards: Vicious 12-lb-test

Most Other Methods: Vicious 6- or 8-lb-test high-vis

SINKERS

Egg sinkers for slow trolling

Tad Poles for fast trolling crankbaits or jigs

MINNOW HOOK

Eagle Claw Rotating 1/0 or 2/0

Floats: Thill 1⁄16-oz floats or stick floats.

JIG HEADS

Muddy Water Baits Whack'em Series ⅛, 3/32, ¼ & 5/16-ounce with 2/0 Eagle Claw hooks

JIG BODIES

Primary: Muddy Water 2.5-inch

Secondary: Muddy Water 2-inch

Smallest: 1-inch tiny body (for black crappie)

Largest: 3.5-inch swim bait with a 3-inch minnow (for Mississippi spawning crappie)

Top Colors in stained/murky water: black-glow; orange-glow; brown-glow; orange-glow; Outlaw color lime-chartreuse

Top Colors in clearer water: Monkey Milk (milky color); blue monkey milk; green monkey milk; white-chartreuse

BAIT RIGS

Slow-Troll Double-Hook Rigs: Capps/Coleman-style with egg sinker between baits. Bottom bait is ⅛- or ¼-ounce jig tipped with a minnow; ⅜-oz egg sinker, and top leader with a minnow hook. Minnow hooks are Rotating 1/0 or 2/0 size. Variations include the distance between hooks and the sinker (12 to 24 inches), size jig (1/16 to ¼-ounce), size sinker (¼- to 1-ounce) and the minnow hook may be modified by adding a solid-plastic body on the shank for color.

Slow-Troll Single Bait Rigs: ¼- or 5/16-ounce jighead.

BAIT RIG HOLDERS

Tackle Buddies with a 2-inch spool (creates less line memory than popular 1-inch types)

NET

Jenko

POLE HOLDERS

Switched to all Driftmaster in 2019

PLANER BOARDS

Off-Shore

LIVE FISH EQUIPMENT

Charlie says, "Keeping fish alive for a tournament starts ahead of time. At the motel, I put in tap water, condition it with Mr. Crappie treatment and cool it down to 65 degrees. I run an oxygenator and Mr. Bubbler. We have air on both sides. I never pull in fresh water because it can have little or no oxygen from the top of the lake. Plus, the pumps are running and crappie don't like current. So now you're stressing them from both bad water coming in and a strong current. It wears them out quickly. The Ranger has good pumps for bass, but they stress crappie.

LIVE BAIT EQUIPMENT

"Keeping a lot of bait alive like we do isn't always easy but we've been having good success with the system we use. Depending upon how many minnows we are going to carry in the boat, we'll use two or three 30-quart Engle Coolers. We use a Mr. Bubbler hooked to a 12-volt system to run air to them. I will split 4 pounds of minnows into three coolers, put a thermometer in each one, make sure they stay cold, never letting them get above 70 degrees with 62 to 65 degrees best," says Charlie.

"In the back of my truck I can carry 20 pounds of minnows with me to a tournament. It really helps that we have Missouri Goldfish for a sponsor. I put two 135-quart coolers with oxygen and aerators. I change water out every third day. I believe one pound is eight or 10 dozen of 2.5- to 3-inch minnows. The dozen per pound is relative to the size of the minnows. When we go to Florida, for example, I want them all to be about ¾- to 1-inch long. To Grenada in spring, I want 3.5- to 4-inch minnows."

SPECIAL THANKS

KEITH "CATFISH" SUTTON

Keith Sutton is at the top of the Who's-Who list of outdoor media. He is a writer, photographer, editor and lecturer with work in more than 350 publications. He served as editor of Arkansas Wildlife for 19 years, the publication of the Arkansas Game & Fish Commission, and has twice been named the Conservation Communicator of the Year. He received the 2019 Legends of the Outdoors Hall of Fame Wade Bourne Outdoor Communicator of the Year Award.

Keith has been a long-time friend and associate in media projects and trips. He is one of the good guys in the business. He provided final proof for this book.

Go to Amazon.com to check out fishing books by Keith Sutton. I promise good reading.

READERS

To you, the reader and fisherman, for buying this book. I hope you use the tips from Charles and Travis to catch more fish.

If you purchased this book from Amazon, please rate/review it. It will help others decide if they should buy it. Thank you.

THE MOST IMPORTANT MESSAGE OF ALL

1 Corinthians 15:57
"But thanks be to God who gives us the victory through our Lord Jesus Christ."

"You can't control how you die but you can control how you will live. God's word says you can have authority, power and victory in your life through Jesus. Don't focus on death that you can't control. Focus on your life and how you will live it. Don't wait to start living. Refuse to live a mediocre life. Step out today with the supernatural power of Jesus and live an amazing life. There are plenty of people that will tell you that you can't have an abundant live, however, God isn't one of them." —Author Barry Young (30 Second Devotional from Amazon)

Made in the USA
Monee, IL
20 May 2024